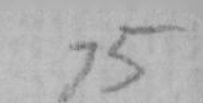

D1214516

garden
design
ILLUSTRATED

garden design

ILLUSTRATED

by JOHN A. GRANT
and CAROL L. GRANT

University of Washington Press
SEATTLE · WASHINGTON

LIBRARY OF CONGRESS
CATALOG CARD NUMBER: 54-12725

COMPOSED ON INTERTYPE FOTOSETTER BY
WESTCOTT & THOMSON, INC., PHILADELPHIA

LITHOGRAPHED BY PHOTOPRESS, INC., CHICAGO

foreword

THIS IS THE third time my wife and I have collaborated in writing a garden book. Our first book, *Trees and Shrubs for Pacific Northwest Gardens,* as its name implies, dealt with plant material for a certain geographic area. Our second, *Pruning Is Simple,* handled a specific technical garden problem but was not confined to just one region. This time we have written on the broad subject of garden design, our aim being to present information that will be of value in any climatic region other than the completely tropical.

This book is intended for all garden lovers, ranging from those who enjoy just looking at a garden to those seriously interested in design and concerned with the actual designing of gardens themselves. I have written from the standpoint of my own experience in the teaching and practice of garden design, and my wife has collaborated from the standpoint of an informed critic, organizer, and editor.

Since most of the gardens illustrated in this book are situated in the Pacific Northwest, an exact imitation of them in other regions with different climatic conditions would not be possible. However, the whole design thesis has been presented as principles of design, with the photographs and drawings illustrating their specific application. Consequently anyone with information as to the plant material that should be used in his locality would be able to utilize these design principles intelligently and effectively.

J. A. G.

acknowledgments

WE WISH TO express our sincere appreciation to all those who have helped to make the publication of this book possible. We are especially indebted to the editors of *House Beautiful* magazine for their cooperation and assistance and for all the photographs and drawings which they have made available to us.

Much of the material in this book was originally published as articles in *House Beautiful,* but that material has now been amplified, revised, and rewritten. Miss Elizabeth Gordon, the editor of *House Beautiful,* urged us to write the series of articles for *House Beautiful.* Her editorial direction and encouragement were invaluable to us.

We also wish to express our special thanks to Mr. Maynard Parker, whose excellent photographs form the bulk of the illustrations in this book, who was at all times most helpful and sympathetic in working to capture with his lens the essence of the garden design.

We wish to acknowledge the permission of Charles Scribner's Sons to quote from Christopher Tunnard's *Gardens in the Modern Landscape.*

We are most grateful to all our friends who have given us so much aid and encouragement in working out the details of the book at its various stages of development from its inception to its completion.

contents

garden
design
ILLUSTRATED

1 introduction

I WAS driving through Oregon early one fall, admiring the brilliant colors of the tumbleweed, which by the first frost had changed to bright crimson, magenta, and purple. I picked a sprig and put it in my buttonhole. Everywhere I stopped—gas stations, restaurants, hotels—I was asked the same question: "What's that pretty flower in your buttonhole?" Apparently no one I talked to had ever seen it before!

The beauty of plants, both weeds and prized horticultural specimens, has been an inspiration to artists, designers, and architects down through the centuries. The ancient Greeks blazoned the acanthus leaf as a decorative architectural motif. The great American prophet of modern architecture, Frank Lloyd Wright, turned for inspiration to the functional structure of flower forms.

Gardeners at the turn of the century showed much awareness of the beauty of plant material. Shortly before there had been a great influx of new and exotic plants into this country. This was the period when arboreta were being established. Ernest H. Wilson became a world-famous figure among plant explorers, and through his prolific writings he popularized the great wealth of plant materials that was being introduced from China and Japan. But gardens were mainly museums. Plants were regimented to form pattern beds that were a reflection of the new vogue for machine-made patterns. Victorian flower beds spotted all over lawns closely corresponded to the whatnots of the Victorian living room loaded with a miscellany of *objets d'art.*

The bedding out system of the late Victorian era has been preserved to the present day in municipal parks and gardens, although it has virtually disappeared from private gardens. But the swing of the pendulum brought the attempt to simplify the design by the use of only a few kinds of plants, which led to monotony and finally to lack of originality. The need is for garden designers to know and appreciate plant material in order to handle it with feeling.

In *Gardens in the Modern Landscape,* Christopher Tunnard, with characteristic pungency, says of the Victorian period, "The mid-nineteenth century saw the arrival of the professor of landscape gardening. . . . Sad to relate, the professor did not make much stir among the English public, who like their landscapists cast in the John Bull mould, and the academician was sent packing to America where he flourished exceedingly, set himself up in universities, and is no doubt partly the cause of the general lack of originality to be found in the landscape art of that country today."

The head of a department of landscape design in one of our universities amazed me by his reply to my statement that the warmer temperate zones had such a thrilling and stimulating abundance of interesting plant material to draw upon, especially the wide range of broad-leaved evergreen shrubs. He said that he didn't think it was particularly stimulating—that for the student to be faced with such an array of plant material was confusing more than anything else. Such a statement from anyone in his position is tragic evidence of how we have lost sight of the importance of plant material in our gardens. Those who hold this view justify the scathing indictment of Christopher Tunnard concerning the lack of original design in American garden architecture. A really sympathetic handling of plant material will result in more genuinely creative garden design. Too many young landscape architects coming out of colleges and universities see no harm in airily proclaiming that they can create a good garden design without a detailed first-hand knowledge of plant material.

In the early 1920's rock gardens became the fad of the hour. The rock garden rage was primarily a resurgence of interest in individual plants and their cultivation. This was a good thing, but the creation of "naturalistic rock outcroppings" was carried to absurd lengths. On Long Island, for example, where there was scarcely a rock to be found, "natural" rock gardens were the vogue. But more than anything else, rock gardening represented an interest in the cultivation of rare and choice alpine and subalpine rock plants, miniature plants of exquisite beauty. Unfortunately choice rock plants require terrifically high maintenance, and by the late 1930's the popular fad had practically died out. The utter impossibility of keeping up a high maintenance garden in wartime was the final blow.

Today we are at the crossroads. There were predictions that the clipped and regimented planting in the New York World's Fair would become a new garden rage, but fortunately the only rage it aroused was in the hearts of lovers of plant material! The fact that this prediction happily failed is evidence of a high potential appreciation of plant material in contemporary American taste. We need to see even more clearly the intrinsic beauty of unregimented plant material. The common belief that modern architecture calls for clipped shrubbery is spurious. Nothing could form a more pleasing and genuine combination than the natural structural simplicity of free-growing plants and the functional simplicity of contemporary architecture. For example, the line pattern of a deciduous tree in winter (each species of tree has its own distinctive branching pattern) can become a vital element in modern garden design. It can be used as an accent point with a bank of shrubs built around it, or it can stand sharply defined against a large panel of a modern building. It doesn't have to be clipped into a cube to become "modern."

The purpose of this book is not to outline a cut-and-dried approach to garden design. The purpose rather is to open up vistas of possibilities through the understanding of naturalistic principles and through a more vivid awareness of the design potential of plant material itself.

approach to garden design

2

"GARDEN" is a word which means something different to everyone. To the horticulturist it is a place for growing plants; to the poet it suggests seclusion, rest, meditation, or perhaps gaiety; to the landscape architect it is a definite unit of design with certain aesthetic and utilitarian functions.

There are many different kinds of gardeners, but they can probably all be grouped into two main divisions—the gardener who is interested mainly in the plants themselves and the gardener who is working for a design. Many of us who love and admire the beauty of the individual plant have gardens that are merely plant collections. Such gardens may give any plantsman a great deal of genuine pleasure and satisfaction. Creating a beautiful living design involves much more than merely growing plants well, but its yield in lasting enjoyment is proportionately greater. As we said in *Trees and Shrubs for Pacific Northwest Gardens,* "it is sometimes true that the love of the plant is lost in a mere intellectual interest in collecting rare specimens without any deep feeling for the beauty of the plants themselves. On the other hand, the gardener who is interested in garden design in a purely intellectual way may lose contact with the real thrill of *growing* plants. The keynote to true enjoyment of plant material, whether the gardener assembles it in the form of a collection or aspires to the artistry of gardening, is the joy of working with growing things. It is the inspiration of the surging upward line of a tree's bare branches in winter, the evidence of an unconquerable will to grow; it is the deep lush green of shade-loving plants growing in a cool corner under a north wall; it is the aromatic foliage of rosemary and lavender basking on a hot dry bank."

But suppose you are more interested in garden design than in the plants. Does that mean that you can ignore the cultural requirements of the plants? Do you believe that you can make plants do what you want them to? Unfortunately that is the trouble with too many garden designs. Garden planners, however, have sometimes been able to get by with this in strictly formal gardens because the plants are secondary to the geometrical pattern and structure of the design. Such tactics always result in grief in an informal garden since the design must be a pleasing combination of contented free-growing plants.

Today good garden design requires both the sympathetic understanding of the plantsman and the design sense of the garden architect.

Two of the most famous landscape designers of the Western world are a Frenchman, LeNotre, and an Englishman, "Capability" Brown. They represent diametrically opposite viewpoints. LeNotre is best known for his grandiose palace gardens at Versailles. He was the founder of what became known as the Grand Style in landscape architecture. When English gardens in the early eighteenth century had become decadent in design, a great reform movement was led by Capability Brown with his "naturalistic" landscape school. He carried the wild, natural scene right up to the walls of castle and mansion, tearing down old garden walls, fences, and hedges, and destroying much that was fine along with much that was bad. Those who tried to stem the tide were dubbed reactionaries. From that time to this there have been ding-dong battles back and forth between the disciples of "formal" and "informal" gardens. The real meaning of the discussion has frequently been obscured in the heat of battle.

Toward the end of the nineteenth century in England Gertrude Jekyll introduced a vigorous new approach which has exerted a great influence on garden design in England and America. Fundamentally her approach was based on a strong affection for all growing things and a deep understanding of their cultural requirements. It was this approach which enabled her to design gardens successfully, and this is what the garden designer of today most needs. She was a pioneer in the art of adapting an arrangement of living material to the site. She insisted that planting should appear to have happened rather than to have been artificially designed.

She left a record in her writings of her experiences, her successes and failures, and above all what she found most pleasing, but she didn't attempt to analyze her work and show how others might achieve the same results. The student of garden design will be better able to produce the harmonious effects which she achieved by feeling and instinct if he learns to analyze the problems, thus discovering certain underlying rules or principles. The study and application of basic principles rather than an exclusive reliance on personal taste are bound to bring about a consistently higher standard of garden design. This tends to lessen the dangerous personal element which limits the success of the artist and garden planner. Analysis clears away the cobwebs of confusion.

Modern architecture in America is far ahead of modern landscape architecture. This is mainly true because so little thought is given to the appreciation of plant material and to the particular soil and site of the garden to be planned. The most interesting and practical design is always made when the garden is the outgrowth of local conditions. It has been shown in architecture that the most frankly appealing house is produced when the building is a logical outgrowth of the site, locality, function, and well-used native and imported materials. A garden so designed is not only more effective and easier to keep up but also it has a permanent value which is bound to increase with time. The superimposed garden, on the other hand, keeps getting more and more difficult to care for, quickly showing neglect.

formal vs. informal

Let us analyze the two types of garden treatment and see what makes a successful example of each. Step first, in imagination, into a formal garden and look at its design. You immediately become conscious of a strong central axis or imaginary line running down the middle of the garden. The design on one side of this dividing line is a duplicate of the other side. This is symmetrical balance. Straight lines, geometric patterns and forms, and pairs of specimens at all important points of interest make up the design. The basis of formal design is a completely symmetrical balance of geometrically shaped beds and architectural objects with the boundaries of the area very strongly marked and defined. In such a design the plant material is subordinated to geometrical pattern. Clipped hedges and clipped specimens of trees or shrubs are used to form and accentuate the structure of the design.

This type of garden design has been used for centuries and under certain conditions can be very satisfying—for example, the garden which is laid out as an architectural extension of a house which has a

Symmetrical pairs are used instead of asymmetrical or occult balance. Solution: remove evergreen, container, and light fixture as indicated, and move the other container for flowers so that it comes in the middle of the panel instead of off to one side. Replace the pair of arborvitae (in foreground) with grass. Plant a loose-growing, spreading shrub in place of the stiff conifer at right of door. Train the pyracantha (left of door) in a loose, open pattern over most of the bare wall space above.

1

2

The two handsome trunks of Douglas fir are part of a large natural grove and not a pair flanking an informal walk, as it might appear. The simplicity of their lines was greatly enhanced by eliminating flower beds around them. Note newly sodded area.

completely symmetrical façade, or a garden which is an entirely segregated area (such as a formal rose garden surrounded by a high hedge). If you don't have either of these conditions, use an informal garden design. Implicit in informal design is asymmetrical balance. The pairs of specimens essential to the formal design have no place in the informal. A pair of trees at an entrance is one of the commonest mistakes in so-called informal gardens. Level areas held up by retaining walls belong to formal treatment, while free-flowing contours tie in with the free-flowing curves of the informal design.

In the formal garden a clear definition of the boundaries of bed areas strengthens the design and accentuates the geometric pattern. This gives greater unity to the formal scene. The border edge, or the edging of beds, however, has no place in the informal garden scene. It is commonly used but only detracts. The edging of beds implies that the design will not hang together without a border planting. The clean-cut lines of the formal treatment should be replaced in the informal treatment by a melting and merging quality. The subtle relationship of the plants themselves and the smooth blending of the curves and contours should hold the design together without the emphasizing lines of borders or edgings.

The garden structure in the formal treatment is architectural, with walls, fences, neatly clipped hedges, beds, and so forth. The garden's principal structure in the true informal treatment is an arrangement of free-growing trees and shrubs planted in irregular groups or drifts—not in lines. These trees and shrubs may be restrained and slightly modified in their growth by proper pruning, but they should never be clipped.

The formal garden's effectiveness depends upon distinct, clean-cut lines—a well-tailored, man-made structure. In the informal garden, which is the commonest type of garden design today, they have no place. The reason that shrubs frequently are clipped is mainly due to ignorance. Actually you can get a shrub to fill almost any space so that when it reaches maturity it will not be too large for the space it is supposed to fill. Well-arranged groupings of free-growing shrubs pleasingly related can bring real beauty to your garden. (See color illustration, page 21.)

summary

formal	*informal*
Symmetrical balance	Asymmetrical balance
All edges sharply defined	Melting and merging
Straight lines of planting	No straight lines of planting
Clipped hedges	Nothing clipped
Man-made levels, retaining walls	Free-flowing contours

what scale does for design

3

There's nothing theoretical about scale. It is the visual relationship of each part of a garden to every other part and to the design as a whole. It is mainly the relationship of size. Once you understand it, you can use it with telling effect. Properly handled, scale creates an illusion of greater space. It establishes distinctive character and produces an illusive quality of atmosphere. If you ignore it, your design falls to pieces because of the disproportionate size of its parts.

Let's begin with the house. The design of the exterior of your house, both as to its component parts and in its relationship to the grounds, is a problem in scale. To give a house of ample proportions a very small front entrance detracts from the effect of the whole. Similarly the entrance walk, steps, and so forth must be in scale with the front door, neither too large nor too small. So, if you have a small "cottage" with a cozy little front entrance, don't give it an important broad sweep of steps. But how are you going to know what is the proper scale? Mentally measure each part for its relationship to neighboring parts and to the scheme as a whole. You will quickly develop a sense of what is the right size. Failure to consider scale is seldom due to lack of ability. It stems from a lack of awareness of its importance. Scale is not a difficult proposition once you are alerted to watching out for it.

Contemporary architectural design makes scale conspicuously important. Faulty scale shows up quickly in the functional, frank use of materials without the distraction of camouflaging surface decorations. (See figures 3 and 4.)

A garden mainly architectural in design—where walls, terraces, and paved areas are an extension of the house itself—must be related in scale to the house. A common violation of this design principle is a house on a steep slope, with a very narrow terrace close to the house. Such a terrace is out of scale with the mass of the house. It looks like a frill tacked around the edge. Proper scale relationship demands a sufficient mass of terrace to support the mass of the house.

When the garden is predominantly architectural, the scale of the architecture determines the scale of the planting. In most gardens, however, the structure is created as much by the plant material as by architectural features, and sometimes more. The design problem becomes one of establishing a scale relationship between the garden planting and the architecture. The key to the whole situation is this—it is always the tree which sets the scale of the planting. Scale in the garden, then, is established by two main determining factors—the architecture or the tree, or more often a combination of both. (See figure 5.)

Here are some of the possibilities. An extremely large building dominant in the landscape leaves little choice but to use a sufficiently large-scale planting (large trees) to cause the house and landscape to become an integrated unit and not a mass with a feeble decoration tacked on. You may do one of three things with a smaller house. (1) Use such a large tree that the house appears even smaller, thus dwarfing it and creating quaintness and charm. (2) Use all small trees and small-scale planting to create the illusion that the house is larger than it actually is. (3) Use a tree or trees of medium height—twenty-five or thirty-five feet—which would allow a small to medium-sized house to appear at its actual size. The third is probably the commonest treatment but less imaginative than either of the other two. Creating an illusion of a larger or smaller house through planting is a phase of landscape design that is rich in exciting possibilities.

One of the best tricks of scale manipulation in the garden is to make the area seem to be a large garden of which only a small portion is visible. Instead of scaling your garden to the dimensions of your lot, make it seem much bigger than the lot. Usually, for city dwellers at least, the house occupies a major portion of the lot. The garden is then out of scale with the house and tends to pull away from it. Where you see the boundaries in a small garden and are conscious of them at all times (because they are sharply defined by an unbroken fence or wall or hedge), you become keenly aware of the smallness of the area. But

3

Restrained planting is in perfect scale with the delicate lines and proportions of the contemporary style of architecture.

4

when the boundaries can be concealed by planting instead of being emphasized, the eye unconsciously tends to assume a continuation of the same type of treatment that it sees in the foreground. Combine this trick with a large-scale planting and you create the illusion that the tiny garden is a small corner of a large estate. (See figure 6.)

This is, of course, by no means the only possible treatment of a small garden. You can do just the reverse if the size of the house permits. If you have a small cottage with a little garden, you may want to surround it with a picket fence. Such a house is on a diminutive scale, and the defining of the garden boundary by the fence emphasizes the smallness of the garden and relates it in scale to the building. A large, imposing house with a small garden enclosed by a picket fence would be dissatisfying because of the failure to maintain proper scale.

Relationship in sizes extends to the smallest part of any design, and so includes all the details of pattern and texture. In working out the choice of plant materials, scale is determined in two ways: (1) by the size of the tree or shrub and (2) by the size of its component parts, i. e., leaves, twigs, branches, and trunk. Suppose you need a fairly large tree for shade and also for scale with the building and the rest of the garden. You can accentuate the large-scale treatment by using a large-leaved tree with strong branching pattern such as catalpa. Or you may modify the scale effect by using a large tree with small leaves and a fine, twiggy branching pattern. Of course, whenever you have an especially large tree to start with, it is essential to use broad-leaved evergreen shrubs that are as bold as possible in texture, although the shrubs must not overpower the house in over-all size.

Similarly, when you pave a certain area, its size may in part be dictated by practical usage. But you still can do much to relate it in scale to the rest of the garden by dividing the space into a pattern and texture. For example, brick set on edge in a herringbone pattern creates a finer texture, and consequently a smaller scale, than brick laid out flat in basket-weave pattern. So your use of paving materials should also take into consideration the question of scale. Different paving materials, varying in coarseness of texture and pattern, and consequently varying from large to small scale, would include smooth cement, fine gravel, crushed brick, brick, tile, concrete blocks, wood rounds, and so forth. A mown lawn is the finest texture in ground cover. Others range in texture from the fine foliage of heather to that of plants like bearberry *(Arctostaphylos)*, ivy, and so on. The differ-

The elm tree planted close to the house is badly out of scale, but as it grows and achieves a more mature size it will be in scale with the house.

5

This huge tree, surrounded by a bank of broad-leaved evergreen shrubs, establishes a very large-scale planting. The small tree in the left foreground should be removed since it conflicts both in scale and sphere of influence.

ence in foliage size is even greater in taller shrubs, ranging from the tiny foliage of heather to the large leaves such as *Prunus laurocerasus* (English laurel), *Mahonia beali, Fatsia japonica,* and *Magnolia grandiflora.*

Finally, in working out groupings of plants, keep the size of each individual group in scale with the whole scheme. Then you achieve a united effect. Remember that you will lose this effect if the groups are either too large or too small.

4 plant material in garden design

CAN YOU have a garden with a permanently pictorial effect the year around—a garden that gives *constant* refreshment charm, delight? The answer, though quite at variance with popular theory, is yes. You *can* have a beautiful garden every day of the twelve months—no matter what climate you live in. The answer is simpler than you think.

The permanently pictorial garden has to have structure—with a capital S. Without it there is nothing left but a few clumps and a sparse scattering of shrubs when the flowers have gone for the season. *A continuously satisfying garden can be built with the plants themselves—if you know how to use plants.*

To create a beautiful picture in your garden you need to know your plant materials in much the same way that an artist has to know his colors and how to use them. You must recognize the "design potential" of trees, shrubs, and flowers. Then use plant material that gives your garden permanent structure—a well-designed skeleton form that stays that way. (See figures 7 and 8.)

First, distinguish between woody plants (trees and shrubs) which have a permanent structure and the herbaceous plants (flowers) which die down to the ground every year. You form the framework of the garden with the trees and shrubs. Use the trees as accents and build around these accent points carefully related shrub masses. Then add groups of softer herbaceous plants to this structure.

The easiest way to understand the structural use of trees and shrubs is to classify them into groups according to their *design function.* Think of them as design elements.

Both trees and shrubs can be subdivided into three groups—deciduous, coniferous evergreen, and broad-leaved evergreen. This gives us six main categories of woody plants, not to mention vines, which are usually deciduous though occasionally broad-leaved evergreen. Each of these groups has a distinct function in the design.

Evergreens give the strongest year-around effect, but there are two types of evergreens and each has a different design function. Have you ever noticed what a strong tone is produced by cedars, pines, firs, spruce, and junipers—the needle-leaved, cone-bearing evergreen trees and shrubs known as evergreen conifers or coniferous evergreens? The other type, the broad-leaved evergreens, is much lighter in tone. When you have looked at a hillside covered with trees of many kinds, you have been aware of the deep dark tones of the evergreen conifers both in the spring, when the new pale foliage was coming out on the maples, birch, and other deciduous trees, and in the fall when the foliage changed color. This contrast was partly caused by a difference in hue—pale yellow greens, yellows, and reds of the deciduous foliage against the deep greens of the conifers. But even in the middle of the summer when the deciduous trees have turned their darkest green you will notice that the conifers still stand out. They appear far darker, almost a black green. This darkness is due to the fact that the coniferous evergreen foliage absorbs a great deal of light, whereas broad-leaved evergreens and deciduous foliage have a higher light reflectivity. Consequently, regardless of the leaf *color,* the conifers always look darker. They often are needed for the strong dark note in the garden scene. However, they must be used sparingly; otherwise they will create a funereal effect. Perhaps your present garden is too somber and needs to be enlivened by eliminating some conifers.

If you stop to look closely at coniferous evergreens, you will find that the dark foliage mass is made up of a pattern of lines. Keep clearly in mind this line pattern of their foliage as well as their darkness, and you will then use them effectively and with restraint.

Broad-leaved evergreen trees and shrubs give the same permanence that coniferous evergreens do, but the surface of their leaves is frequently glossy and reflects more light. They are never somber. Consequently broad-leaved evergreens can be used effectively in much greater quantities than conifers. There is wide variation in the size of their foliage, from the tiny leaves of the smallest heathers to the great handsome leaves of the evergreen magnolia *(Magnolia grandiflora),*

Easy grace and simplicity are achieved by gently rolling contours, curving path, and closely related sequences of broad-leaved evergreen foliage accented by flowering trees.

English laurel *(Prunus laurocerasus),* and large-leaved rhododendrons. The term broad-leaved evergreens thus refers not only to evergreens with big, broad leaves but also to a full range of foliage sizes from the smallest to the largest. It is used to distinguish trees and shrubs of this class from the needlelike or fernlike foliaged coniferous evergreens. Coniferous evergreen foliage is a pattern of lines whereas broad-leaved evergreen foliage is a pattern of planes. Broad-leaved evergreen shrubs make up the most important single group of structural plant material. There is seldom a garden that could not be improved by a more generous and understanding use of them. (See figures 9 and 10.)

The all-important design feature of broad-leaved evergreen shrubs is the texture and pattern of their foliage mass. One with small individual leaves creates a fine-textured foliage mass, one with large leaves, a relatively coarse texture. Use related sequences of foliage size and pattern.

Many broad-leaved evergreens are not hardy in colder climates. So the warmer the climate the greater the wealth of broad-leaved evergreens from which to draw.

Deciduous foliage (which drops each winter) is necessary to the garden picture even in the warmest sections. It provides added interest with its seasonal color changes. In addition, a spectacular display of bloom at some period during the growing season makes some of the deciduous shrubs quite indispensable. The garden in which deciduous shrubs are used exclusively will have a light and airy structure. Such a garden, however, will be weak, since it does not have the strength and permanence which evergreens impart. Deciduous trees and shrubs are important structural materials, but in all except the coldest climates the deciduous shrubs play second fiddle to the broad-leaved evergreens. Deciduous shrubs are especially useful as a direct background for the herbaceous plants, and deciduous trees make an important accent rising up through a bank of broad-leaved evergreen foliage. A large deciduous tree standing alone may be the dominant note in your garden, with the line pattern of its branches forming the keynote of the design.

Next consider the lawn, which is very much an element in the design. A large area of fine texture is needed to set off smaller areas of more vigorous pattern and texture. Grass lawn has become the commonest and most conventional of all ground-cover treatments in the average garden. But don't assume that grass is the only possible ground-cover material to use. True, it is often the best practical solution since

The modern picture window, which brings the garden into the house, makes it necessary to have a permanently pictorial effect.

The same window, looking in instead of out.

it can stand up to fairly heavy traffic. But where climate and soil conditions permit, it is sometimes very effective to use huge sheets of low-growing heather, which fulfill this same basic design requirement—that of producing a large area of fine texture. Similarly other plant materials are often better than mown grass on a very steep bank, in dense shade, or in other soil and moisture conditions not ideal for most grasses. This point is stressed because the thinking on this subject is too frequently stereotyped, and it is often assumed that a lawn is the only ground-cover material. Instead, consider the problem from the aspects of both practicality and design. If you need an area for useful living space, first decide whether you want lawn or paving. Then decide just how much of this space is needed for actual use. For the rest of the area choose the material whose texture will best fit in with the design. In other words, be willing to think in terms of something other than lawn as a solution for your ground-cover problem. (See figures 11 and 12.)

The simple classification of plant material just described is a great help to the garden designer, but there is another vital factor which must always be considered. To think of plant material just as so many examples of line pattern, sequence of texture, color, and form is to forget the most vital part of garden design—naturalistic character. It is essential to treat plant materials as living, growing individuals. Plants growing together under similar climatic and cultural conditions will be found to have certain characteristics in common. For instance, the shady woodland plants frequently have a combination of rather light yellow-green delicate foliage, openly distributed along the stems, and usually small flowers with a white or cream to pale yellow color range. Meadow plants may have similar foliage although often slightly heavier and denser, but they frequently have quite showy flowers, both larger and brighter in color than those of woodland plants. The combined effect of these hard-to-define characteristics of plants—whereby an experienced plantsman can immediately tell whether a plant comes from shady woodland or sunny meadow, from swampy marsh or arid desert—indicates generally what is meant by naturalistic character. In order to make the best use of plant material in the garden, it should be placed so that the plants are related in naturalistic character. The longer you work with plants the more you will find that if you place together plants which grow well together the more satisfactory your design will be. Therefore, a study of plant ecology—that is, a study of plants in relation to their environment—is most important to the artist-gardener.

9

Bold pattern and texture of *Viburnum davidi* and *Raphiolepis ovata* greatly enhance this showroom window.

10

Rhododendron carolinianum (right foreground), *Viburnum davidi* (middle foreground), and *Rhododendron californicum* (behind *Viburnum*) make a combination of pleasing textures with the pattern and line of the stepping stone path.

A sheet of heather is often a useful substitute for a lawn and may be planned to give a sequence of flower color that extends throughout the year.

12

Drifts of heather and other ground cover material, with a pattern of paths, provide the principal structure of this area.

Grouping plants according to naturalistic character also helps in giving you a basically good color scheme. Desert foliages are characteristically a woolly gray-green—sagebrush, for example. At the other extreme, lush bog plants have vivid yellow-green foliage. If you group your plants in such a way that those of similar cultural requirements are kept together, it will not only simplify the design of your garden but also magically reduce the work of upkeep.

summary

Classify your plant material according to its use in the garden design. First, select woody plant material—trees and shrubs—to form the garden structure, the trees serving as accent points with shrubs massed around them. Then clothe and soften this structure with the herbaceous plants—annuals, biennials, perennials, and bulbs.

To create a garden structure with plant material, remember the following points:

1. Consider trees the accent points.
2. Use just a very small percentage of coniferous evergreen foliage for strength, weight, and accent.
3. Use as large a percentage of broad-leaved evergreen shrubs as your climatic conditions permit. Relate them in a sequence of foliage size and pattern.
4. Use the lighter, softer deciduous foliages in subordination to the broad-leaved evergreen foliage masses to give a note of seasonal change and as a background for herbaceous plants.
5. Group your plants according to their cultural requirements. Then they are much more likely to look well together.

5 trees—the keynote of garden design

IF YOU know what a tree means to the design of your garden, then you will know how to select a tree and how to place it.

Did you know that a tree is an accent point in your garden? It is. And perhaps that is why your neighbor's garden has looked too "busy" to you—it is too full of accent points! Your neighbor has not learned the important difference between the effect of a tree and a shrub. The clearly defined trunk of a tree gives it a definite character which sets it apart from shrubs and makes it a distinct and separate unit. It becomes an accent point in the design in contrast to the blended masses produced by the shrubs. Just as a schoolboy sometimes scatters punctuation marks liberally through his writing, in the same way some gardeners plant far too many trees, with the result that the composition is broken up, producing a spotty, restless effect. Because each tree is an accent point, you can use only a few. (See figure 13.)

You would not want your garden to look just like a nursery sales yard with its miscellaneous jumble of attractive trees and shrubs assembled in a collection without any attempt at design. Yet this is the way too many gardens look—collections of plant material with no harmonious relationship, no pleasing blending of parts.

Maybe it seems like an academic abstraction to say that the difference between a tree and a shrub is that a tree has a clearly defined trunk while a shrub branches from the base. But this difference is not nearly so abstract as you might think. Even though the distinction is a subtle one to the untrained eye, anyone will notice the difference between a garden in which trees are used with restraint and one in which they have been scattered around indiscriminately. So this brings us to one of the important simple secrets of successful garden design. *Don't use too many trees.*

Once you are committed to using only a few trees you will need to have some way of narrowing down the wide range of enchanting and dramatic trees from which you can choose. The first important design factor to consider in making your choice is scale. The size of a tree sets the scale of your garden picture. A full-grown "tree" in a miniature alpine scene in a rock garden may be not more than two feet tall and still be just as important and dominant as a mighty hundred-foot oak in a landscape set to a correspondingly larger scale. (See figure 14.)

When you choose the trees for your garden, notice the relationship between (1) the size of the total area of the garden, (2) the size of the house (which is usually part of the garden scene), and (3) the size of the trees. Suppose your house seems too large for its setting and you want to give it a more gracious aspect. A very large tree will dominate the scene and reduce the apparent size of the house, soften it and at the same time hold its own against an otherwise overpowering architectural mass. Or if you have a modest cottage that you want to make more impressive, use several smaller trees. Watch, though, that you do not choose too tiny a tree. If you do, you will find that it will look smaller than it actually is. In other words, it will appear diminutive or out of scale.

If you are fortunate enough to have a fine old shade tree on your property, let it determine the scale of the garden. A huge tree demands a large-scale plan. The trick in this case is to design the garden as though it were a small part of a very much larger scene, thus tying in with the greater scale set by the tree—as though the area were a big garden or an extensive estate, and you are just seeing one corner of it.

The area of the garden which is dominated by any given tree might be called the tree's "sphere of influence." Each tree or group of trees of one kind should dominate its own sphere of influence. (See drawings on facing page.) The drawings show an imaginary line which indicates a tree's sphere of influence. To apply this in your own case, find out from some reliable source the ultimate height of the tree you want to use. Then calculate that that tree's sphere of influence is a circle with a radius equal to the ultimate height of the tree. Thus a thirty-five-foot tree, such as one of the flowering crabapples or cherries, has a sphere of influence of thirty-five feet in any direction from the trunk of the

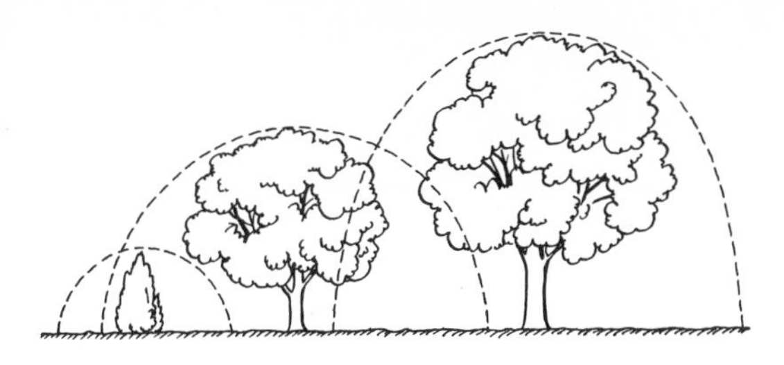

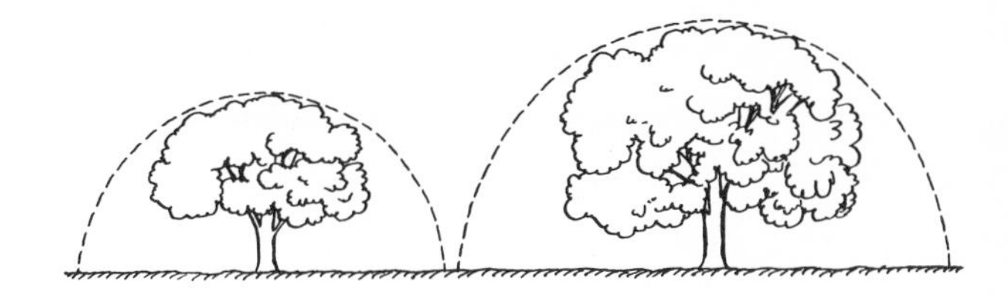

Avoid overlapping spheres

If you plant trees too close to each other, they give a cluttered effect. The dotted line enclosing each tree in the sketch indicates its particular sphere of influence. It is determined by making a circle with a radius equal to the ultimate height of the tree. Do not allow these dotted lines—that is, the trees' spheres—to overlap one another as they are doing here.

Treat trees as accents

If you keep in mind that every tree is an accent point, you will understand the necessity of allowing plenty of space for each one you plant in your garden. Here two trees of different sizes are rightly spaced so that they do not encroach upon each other. Note that the dotted lines indicating their spheres of influence touch at base but do not overlap.

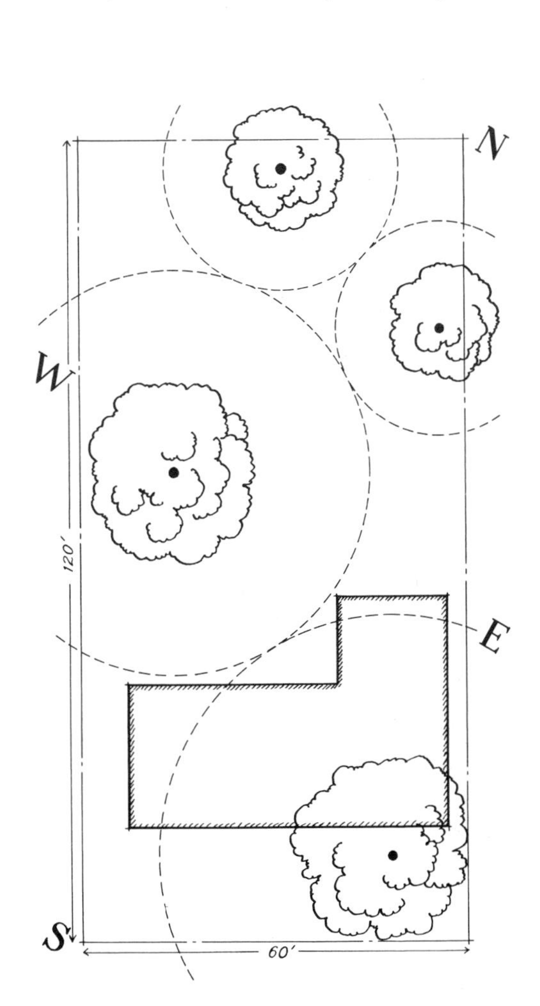

Tree planting plan

The average city lot (60 x 120 feet) can accommodate about four trees—two medium size and two small ones. Dotted lines show spheres of influence.

13

This pretty flowering crab, with clearly defined trunk, accentuates and sets the scale of the planting in a small suburban garden.

A miniature spruce tree sets the scale in an alpine garden scene.

14

In spite of the fact that only the trunk of the dogwood (*Cornus nuttalli*) appears in the picture (left foreground), yet it dominates the area and unifies the design in which the shrub masses and the curve of the lawn are directly related to the position of the tree, showing the design significance of a tree trunk.

A lawn area carved out of a piece of naturalistic woodland in which no one tree is an accent point.

tree. Say that the next tree you might want to use has an ultimate height of twenty feet. Then the minimum distance from the trunk of the thirty-five-foot tree to the trunk of the twenty-foot tree would be fifty-five feet. It might be preferable to have them even farther apart.

An assortment of little trees tucked around a larger one clutters its sphere of influence, upsets the scale, and takes away the feeling of restful spaciousness that is essential to a pleasing design. On the average-sized suburban lot, you can't very well use more than four or five trees effectively. And if one of the trees which you do use is a large one, you may find yourself limited to two or three in the whole garden—or possibly only one if the tree is a huge old specimen. In other words, if you have a hundred-foot tree on a hundred-foot lot, its sphere of influence will cover the entire lot.

There is an exception to this rule which might at first glance seem to be a contradiction. Suppose your house is situated in a little piece of naturalistic woodland—and you have had the good sense not to chop down all the native trees. They are mostly of one kind and have grown together for a number of years. Their tops have formed a canopy overhead, but the trunks are bare of branches to a considerable height. Here you have a woodland area which is an integrated unit. Instead of being conscious of the trees as separate and distinct accent points, you find the trunks are more like pillars holding up a ceiling. Trees which grow together in this way in a natural association form a simple naturalistic unit. (See figure 16.) You lose this simplicity and get an effect of spotty accentuation if you introduce other trees that are not related in character or in scale to the existing growth. It is better to supplement this native growth with shrubs than other trees.

You can produce a similar woodland effect by planting two or three different kinds of trees in a broad, over-all pattern of tree trunks. It is a good plan to make a natural association of native trees in your local area the basis of such a combination. Planting an over-all pattern of trees is only satisfactory when you are consciously planning for a shady woodland garden with its particular limitations as well as its advantages. More often the garden planting that meets the usual home owner's needs involves a type of treatment that is less strictly naturalistic. It is frequently more desirable to have three or four distinctive individual trees as accent points and to build the planting around them.

Working out the choice of trees for your garden along these lines, you can readily see that the selection and placing of trees is based upon a few fundamental principles, and that instead of making a random choice you let your decision be governed by the following principles:

1. Keep prominently in mind that every tree is an accent point. Then you will be careful not to use too many trees.
2. Choose the trees that are just the right size to be in scale with the scene in which you plan to place them.
3. Do not let any tree encroach upon another's sphere of influence.

The number of trees which you can use in building the garden structure is thus automatically determined. One tree might dominate a whole garden. Another garden the same size might have two or three slightly smaller trees, while still another might have as many as four or five, some of moderate size and some quite small. In other words, there is considerable freedom of choice within the framework of these simple basic rules.

6 trees—deciduous and broad-leaved evergreen

A DECIDUOUS tree is most often the keynote to the whole design in gardens of the cool temperate zone. In the warm temperate zones, such as the southern United States, there are a few broad-leaved evergreen trees which are of garden importance. In subtropical zones the broad-leaved evergreen trees almost completely replace the deciduous.

The special design characteristic of a *deciduous* tree is the line pattern of its branches. For example, the Lombardy poplar forms a pattern (as well as an outline) of vertical lines, sharply ascending. The weeping willow, though round-headed in form, also has vertical lines, but gracefully descending. The first one carries your eye upward, and the latter carries your eye downward. Each type of branching pattern may be used with dramatic effect if you have just the right spot for it and the design demands it.

Remember how effective a weeping willow is when planted by the side of a lake, pond, or stream. The line of the branches, carrying the eye downward to its reflection, is a particularly happy design use of the tree. In addition, it fits in with the tree's cultural requirements, namely, the desire to have its toes down in the water.

The upright line of a Lombardy poplar is a dramatic form—an exclamation point in the landscape. Such a tree would be effective as a vertical line in contrast to a long, low-lying mass of farm buildings set in flat, low country. Occasionally a formal garden may require a slender columnar form in a deciduous tree of much smaller scale than a Lombardy poplar. There is a Japanese hybrid cherry, *Ama-no-gawa,* which is an excellent choice. Even though you have a strong urge to use such dramatic extremes as a vertical upright or a weeping tree, be very cautious about using one unless you are sure you have just the spot that demands it. In other words, keep in mind that usually you won't have the right spot to use either of these extremes in branching pattern. In most gardens you will achieve a much more harmonious effect by using intermediate patterns—either gracefully overarching, gently upward-curving, or horizontal.

Learn the "architecture" of deciduous trees. If you can appreciate the exquisite beauty of the line pattern of a tree's bare branches sharply etched against a winter's sky, you have the fundamental understanding for selecting a deciduous tree around which to build a garden design. (See figure 17.) You won't have any difficulty in deciding what to use if you once become conscious of the direction of line which a deciduous tree's branching pattern gives to the garden picture. Have you observed the beauty of a fine old oak with its great mushroom head of upward-sweeping branches with their gnarled and twisted elbows? Does not such a tree give a sense of intriguing character and satisfying strength? Every tree of a given species has a certain typical outline and pattern of bare branches against the winter skies. A tree that is slightly arching should be grouped with broad-leaved evergreen shrubs that have a graceful droop to their foliage. A tree having an upright tendency looks better with broad-leaved evergreen shrubs whose foliage follows somewhat the same direction and feeling. The choice of both the tree and the shrubs would depend upon whether an upright, horizontal, or drooping line was required at a particular point in your garden picture.

To build out and down from the corner of a house in order to tie its vertical line into the horizontal line of the ground, use a tree and shrub grouping with an arching line pattern and foliage texture. On the other hand, if at the far end of the property you wish to lift the eye toward an interesting view—perhaps a vista of mountains in the distance—use a vigorous lifting line in both tree and shrubs. Use a tree with a vertical line only where you feel the need of carrying the eye directly upward. A vertical tree placed in a small enclosed area usually has a disturbing effect—it carries your eye upward and then lets it stop abruptly. Use a weeping tree only where there is a definite reason for carrying the eye downward. Even a beautiful weeping cherry set out in the middle of a level lawn loses all its charm and looks like a pudding basin turned upside down.

Winter snows accentuate the beauty of the "architecture" of the deciduous tree.

You cannot judge the branching pattern of a tree by the appearance of a very young specimen. For this reason it is not satisfactory to base your selection upon young trees which you find in the nursery. Find out how a mature specimen of a certain species or variety looks and how long it may take to achieve this effect. Many trees which have a gracefully arching pattern in maturity look slightly awkward when young because the branches have a tendency to ascend at a sharp angle. As they increase in age and weight they gradually lower themselves and so come to have a very pleasing line. Some trees never do develop a gracefully branching pattern. The well-known Japanese flowering cherry, *Kwanzan,* also known as *Hi-zakura,* is a very awkward tree from the standpoint of branching pattern, although it is spectacular in bloom with its huge, pink double flowers. Other less well-known varieties, equally lovely in bloom, have far more interesting habits of growth. The beautiful *Shirotae* (sometimes called *Mt. Fuji*) creates a vigorous horizontal line with a profusion of lovely, white pendent flowers. The soft pink *Shiro-fugen* is almost as good, and the dainty pale pink *Shogetsu* is gracefully arching, its branches weighed down with the hanging masses of pink double flowers. Varieties of *Prunus subhirtella,* the spring cherry, are quite different in their pattern, with pink twigs and branchlets more like a birch.

Some trees have thick branches that do not diminish rapidly in size toward the tips. Trees with large individual leaves such as catalpa, paulownia, and figs have stout twigs and branchlets to support the heavy foliage. Mature specimens of many oaks often have stout, gnarled curving branches that form a pattern and structure of great strength and vigor. Such trees are best allowed to develop as *individual specimens.* Other trees, such as birches, have branches that rapidly divide into slender branchlets and lacy twigs. These are more attractive *planted in groups.* (See figure 18.)

A broad-leaved evergreen tree, as a mature specimen, has a clearly discernible branching structure throughout the year, even though this branching structure is clothed with evergreen foliage. The design effect in the garden is usually helped by thinning the branching structure slightly so that the line pattern of the tree is emphasized and more light and air are let in. Broad-leaved evergreen trees of this class include the live (evergreen) oaks, the evergreen magnolia, *(Magnolia grandiflora),* and the madrona *(Arbutus menziesi)* of the Pacific Northwest. (See figure 19.)

18

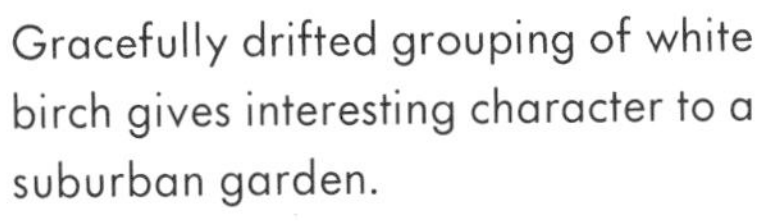

Gracefully drifted grouping of white birch gives interesting character to a suburban garden.

19

The madrona (*Arbutus menziesi*) often makes a handsome specimen tree.

20

The fruiting apple is pleasingly related to a bold grouping of rhododendrons.

To make an intelligent, practical choice you must know something about a tree's garden behavior. Some of the best large shade trees for a garden will be found among the oaks and the birches. Elms, which have a beautiful, fountainlike branching structure, are impossible *garden* trees because they are such greedy feeders. Their voracious fibrous roots close to the surface of the ground rob other trees, shrubs, and flowers of all available food and moisture. The roots will cover an area in a radius of at least fifty feet and often many times that distance. Although elms are, therefore, unsuitable garden trees, they are eminently desirable and practical for planting in large sweeps of landscape, in large parks, or any areas where they do not provide too much competition for other growth.

Poplars and willows are almost equally bad in this respect and their roots are especially destructive to drains and sewers. Even the handsome weeping willows should not be planted except where there is ample moisture in the ground.

Don't plant a weeping willow beside an artificial concrete pool which has been built in dry ground. The tree would soon take over the surrounding garden area with a mass of hungry and thirsty roots. The correct selection in such a case would be a weeping cherry, which prefers well-drained soil. You would then have a well-behaved weeping tree and also a lovely display of blossom in the spring. A moisture-loving tree, like a willow, in dry ground will try to make up for the lack of water by continuously dropping its older leaves all summer long. The result is a constantly untidy garden.

Large trees which cast very dense shade are unsuitable for gardens because it is extremely difficult to grow any satisfactory planting underneath them. Trees of this type include beeches, chestnuts, horse chestnuts, planes, and some of the maples. Where huge specimens of such trees already exist, it is usually better to take advantage of them rather than to try to replace them with something else that may take many years to achieve the same size and give the same degree of maturity to the landscape. There is nothing like a well-developed, large specimen of deciduous tree to give an almost immediate effect of maturity to a new house and garden.

The area under dense shade trees cannot be used for most of the choicer plants, but you can plant the sturdiest and most shade-resistant evergreen ground covers—such as pachysandra, sarcococca, salal,

English ivy, or ferns—and a few shade-resistant shrubs like aucuba and skimmia, or you can pave the area.

You can simplify your garden problems if you choose a tree that will adjust to the soil conditions you have to offer it. For instance, you may want to plant a beautiful flowering cherry in soil that is heavy clay. The practical thing to do, however, is to plant a flowering crabapple, which will be a very acceptable substitute. The crabapple will thrive in a heavy, moisture-retentive soil while the cherry would only be miserable and would possibly die out after a few years.

Many flowering crabapples have a graceful, overarching branching habit that fits readily into the garden picture. Branches kept sufficiently sparse by judicious thinning and summer pruning attain the beauty sometimes seen in a picturesque old apple tree. An ordinary apple tree is lovely in flower, fruit, and branching pattern—and, in addition, you have the fruit to eat. Many improved varieties of fruit trees are handsome flowering trees and may be incorporated in the garden planned primarily for aesthetic effect. (See figure 20.)

Do not overlook two of the most spectacular of flowering trees, the western dogwood (*Cornus nuttalli*) and the smaller eastern species (*Cornus florida*). Mature specimens have a superb branching pattern with the flowers held in a horizontal plane.

There is a wide range of small- to medium-sized flowering trees especially suitable for the average garden from the cultural standpoint. The great majority of these will be found among the genera *Prunus* and *Malus*. *Prunus* includes the flowering and fruiting cherries, plums, peaches, almonds, and apricots. *Malus* includes the apples and crabapples. Vine maple, laburnum, hawthorne, mountain ash, rose acacia, Judas tree, maidenhair tree, and Spindleberry are some of the others in the small- to medium-sized range.

The best garden trees prefer a deep, light, well-drained soil. Their roots strike down deeply instead of feeding on the surface. A heavy soil is a disadvantage because it often discourages the trees from striking down with their roots. Always cultivate deeply in heavy soils before planting garden trees. If the subsoil is clay or hardpan, dig a hole five or six feet wide and not less than three feet deep and remove the impervious hardpan. You must also ensure adequate drainage to a depth of not less than four feet.

Finally, remember that before you choose a tree you must find out how big it will grow. Too often we see the tragedy of a tree that has outgrown its position and has been brutally cut back until it has lost all its natural grace and charm. Decide just how large you want a tree to be and then choose one that will grow to that size but will not exceed it.

7 trees—coniferous evergreen

Conifers are the exclamation marks in landscaping. They are strong and dark and give vigor to your garden. Use them with restraint. If scattered about indiscriminately they do more to break up a garden design than any other wrong planting. A series of columnar conifers standing like a row of exclamation points across the front of a house adds nothing to the architecture of the house and still less to the garden. (See figures 21 and 22.) Pairs of conifers scattered about are the bane of informal garden plantings. But a fine specimen, well placed against a brick or stone building, can give needed strength, character, and unity to the design.

Coniferous evergreen foliage is made up of a pattern of lines. These lines are sometimes long, strong, and sharply etched, as in the case of long-needled pines, which are coarse-textured in effect. Contrasted with this, the lines of the foliage of many of the junipers and chamaecyparis (retinospora) are short and fine, giving a softer effect. The foliage lines are arranged in curving patterns in the cedar type of foliage. The foliage patterns of yews are intermediate in vigor, but they are especially dark in color which gives them proportionately greater weight. However, almost all these needle-leaved evergreens have a dull, individual leaf surface, and from a little distance the strongly light-absorbent masses of the needles contain deep shadows. Conifers with the softest foliage give a surprising impression of darkness and strength when viewed from a distance.

Conifers are often featured in foundation plantings. A large brick or stone structure demands the maximum strength of planting, such as the vigorous texture of the longer-needled pines. (See figure 23.) Where there is less brick or stone, but the strength and darkness of a conifer are still called for, you can utilize the distinctive character of one of the interesting types of cedar foliage. Where even less vigor is demanded, the softness of juniper foliage may add just the touch that your scene needs. Evergreen conifers may be used to some extent with more massive frame structures.

A foundation planting should tie the vertical lines of the house down to the horizontal lines of the ground. These vertical lines are most apparent at the corners, especially at the outermost corners of the building. Consequently the planting at these corners should soften, not accentuate, them. This is *not* the place to use a pyramidal or columnar evergreen conifer, which would only emphasize the vertical line. Trees with horizontal lines are usually most desirable for base planting. For any planting other than the most strictly formal you will get the most pleasing effect by choosing varieties that are irregular in outline. Train them in such a way as to emphasize their irregularity. In other words, prune, *do not clip*, them. (See figure 24.)

Most conifers are trees rather than shrubs. That is, they have clearly defined trunks, even though some of the dwarf horticultural forms (discussed later) are miniature trees not more than a few inches high. The smallest coniferous trees are especially effective in the rock garden. (See figure 25.) A number of the junipers and one or two forms of yew are, or may be, treated as shrubs. The prostrate junipers, especially, are valuable with bold naturalistic rock outcroppings or on steep banks. They do not constitute a definite accent point in the design.

The dwarf and semidwarf conifers have been long in coming into their own in English and American gardens, although for many centuries the Japanese have realized their value and used them effectively. This does not mean trees that are artificially dwarfed by starving and painstaking pruning, for which Japan is famous, but trees or shrubs which remain dwarfed under normal garden conditions. There are hundreds of these true dwarfs to choose from. Mature specimens graduate in size from three or four inches to ten feet or more in height. Dwarf conifers are usually most readily obtainable from nurseries which specialize in rock garden plants. They may seem expensive, but actually they are much better value than cheap conifers and continue to increase in value the longer you have them.

The dwarf forms originate in one of three ways:

BEFORE

21

AFTER: Notice softness of planting and elimination of coniferous evergreen exclamation points.

22

The strength and darkness of a sprawling Japanese black pine give pleasing character to the transition between the handsome Roman brick wall and the wood. The coarse texture of the long needles is strong enough to hold its own with the weight of the masonry.

23

Clipping has completely destroyed the beauty of these conifers.

24

1. There will occur in a batch of seedlings a wide variation in habit and form of some conifers. In exceptional cases there will be a conspicuously dwarf form which retains this habit to maturity.
2. High up in certain large, well-developed specimens of Norway spruce, or Japanese cryptomeria, or some of the pines a congested twiggy growth will form into a curious head known as a "witch's broom." Cuttings taken from this "broom" and rooted or grafted usually retain the dense, slow-growing habit of the "broom," and another dwarf form results. There are over sixty different dwarf forms of Norway spruce, mature specimens varying in size from a few inches high up to fifteen or twenty feet, as contrasted with 200-foot normal trees. There is also considerable variation in habit of growth; some are conical with long, slender lines, some short, dumpy pyramids—an endless variety of inverted, pudding-basin shapes and several distinct weeping and prostrate forms. The dwarf spruces are very valuable in the rock garden, but their use in general landscape planting is strictly limited because of their stiffness and hard, crisp outline.
3. There is a group of dwarfs known as juvenile forms. If you have ever noticed the seedling of one of the cedarlike conifers such as arbor vitae or Lawson cypress, you will recall that it has a feathery foliage quite distinct from its mature foliage produced a few months later. These seedling leaves are sometimes known as juvenile foliage. In rare instances the distinct juvenile foliage of some seedlings is not replaced by mature foliage, and thus is originated another type of dwarf, known as a *juvenile form.* There are several fine juvenile forms of the Lawson cypress or Port Orford cedar *(Chamaecyparis lawsoniana)* and also numerous forms of some of the Japanese chamaecyparis, commonly known in nurseries as retinospora. Dwarfs of this type are especially useful because their soft outline and loose growth make them blend more readily with accompanying planting, whereas those that constitute a sharp accent, if used at all freely, give a restless feeling to the design. Juvenile forms, without exception, prefer light to moderate shade. They never really thrive in full sun and dry conditions.

Most conifers grow well in watered gardens. The majority of them

A miniature juniper (*Juniperus communis compressa*) forms a subalpine forest in this make-believe alpine meadow. Inspired design for an alpine garden must always establish such a miniature scale so that the tiny alpine plants may appear to good advantage.

25

A Douglas fir is handsome rising out of a well-designed patio.

26

prefer ground that is at least moderately moist. A few—for example, some species of pine and juniper—are natives of dry rock ledges, and thus lose their character and become rank and lush in growth if given ordinary watered garden conditions.

The full range of sizes in the coniferous evergreen trees—all the way from the wee miniatures to huge forest trees—provides many conifers of intermediate size particularly valuable in garden planting. With such a variety from which to choose, there is every reason to select conifers of just the right size for any given spot and to choose one with the required design characteristic. Deodar cedar *(Cedrus deodora)* and the hemlocks provide a good illustration of the trouble that results if you don't consider mature size. They are fascinating trees when small, with an irregular outline of gracefully arching branches. Consequently they are frequently planted in small gardens, although they will ultimately attain a height of 100 to 150 feet, with a spread of branches at the base of as much as fifty feet across. So you can see that such a tree is going to be too large to plant under your window! It's quite easy to fall into the mistake of thinking, "Oh, well, it probably won't get big for a long time and then we can get something else." You might just as well start properly—plant a tree that will not exceed its position and then observe your planting grow in beauty and distinction year after year.

Trees and shrubs that have been clipped back to abnormal size for many years frequently become greatly weakened and fall an easy prey to pests and diseases. That is one reason why so many evergreen conifers which have been clipped for years look so unattractive.

Wherever large conifers take up too much space in the garden and you want to keep them, don't chop the tops off. Begin removing the lower branches of the good specimens of these large trees and allow the tops to develop. Never make them unsightly by cutting off their tops and clipping the side branches back. The ground underneath will be hard to plant, so this may not be ideal from an ardent gardener's point of view. However, you can plant it with a tough ground cover or pave it. (See figure 26.)

8

broad-leaved evergreen shrubs

Blooming shrubs give great satisfaction when they are in bloom. But how they contribute to the over-all garden design the other eleven months of the year—when they are not in bloom—is what really matters.

That's why the big group of broad-leaved evergreens is so popular with people who want their properties to look attractive the year around. That's why rhododendrons, camellias, mountain laurel, evergreen azaleas, and hollies get a big display in nursery catalogs and why they play such a prominent part in good gardens in the climatic zones where they thrive. But—and it's an important but—there is a basic misunderstanding about the proper use of broad-leaved evergreens. If you are choosing a rhododendron, chances are ten to one you will give first thought to the color of the flowers. You will say, "I want a good *pink* rhododendron." Actually what you should say is, "I want a rhododendron with broad, handsome foliage to blend with other broad-leaved evergreens of smaller foliage."

At first you may be irked by this attitude. For it is very human to think about plants in terms of their bloom. But the truth is you should think first about foliage size, shape, pattern, and color, for they are the things that make broad-leaved evergreens effective the year around. And you can probably still have just the flower color you want. If you want high pictorial value all the time, you cannot lay all the emphasis on the color scheme of the flowers. For the shrub will be in bloom, at most, from three weeks to a month. What about its appearance the other eleven months of the year?

The light-reflecting nature of the broad-leaved evergreens makes us conscious of the size and shape of the individual leaf. And the way the leaves are arranged on the branches gives a definite pattern to the textured mass of the shrub as a whole. Every shrub of a given kind has a unique pattern and texture of its own. A shrub with large individual leaves necessarily creates a coarse-textured effect, one with small leaves a fine-textured effect. The most desirable way to combine these foliages in the garden is to use them in a carefully related sequence of foliage sizes. You should have the same difference between the first foliage size and the second as between the second and the third, and the third and the fourth, and so on down the line.

It is very much like walking down a flight of stairs. If the steps are all the same size you can walk down comfortably without tripping. The same thing holds true in grouping foliage sizes so that the stepping in foliage is *visually comfortable.* If the stepping is approximately the same amount all down the line, a much more comfortable feeling will result, and you will gain an effect of harmonious blending. (See figure 27.)

If you want to begin with a conifer, decide on how coarse- or bold-textured it should be, placing it as a specimen or accent. Then build around it a sequence of foliages, using the coarsest or largest leaf next to the conifer and diminishing the foliage size as you work away from the conifer. (See figures 28 and 29.) The first basic principle in the design of these foliage combinations is to use a comparatively small area of vigorous texture set off by a large area of fine texture. There is another way of stating the application of this basic principle, which is really an elaboration of it. You begin by using a small quantity of coarsest texture—one broad-leaved evergreen shrub with leaves of the largest size that you plan to use. Then with each decrease in foliage size you proportionately increase the quantity of foliage of smaller size. Therefore, as you progressively and rhythmically decrease the coarseness of texture, the quantity of each shrub of finer texture rapidly increases. In other words, you end up with practically the same thing as stated in the first rule, namely, that a small area of bold texture is set off by a comparatively large area of fine texture, *with a rhythmic sequence (or gradation) of texture in between,* proportionately increasing in quantity. Note that even the largest-leaved deciduous shrubs are not so strong in texture as the small-leaved, broad-leaved evergreens such as *Ilex crenata* or box. Thus you may use a comparatively large-leaved deciduous shrub right next to a small-leaved, broad-leaved evergreen, and the effect will still be a progressively diminishing strength of foliage texture.

One possible texture combination would be to start with a pine, and place a hybrid rhododendron with large leaves next to it. Then, if you want to end the sequence with heather, which has a very small leaf, you could use Oregon grape, evergreen huckleberry, pernettya, and heather for a sequence. Another combination would be rhododendron, Oregon grape, *Pieris japonica,* evergreen huckleberry, *Azalea macrantha,* pernettya, and heather. This gives an example of pattern and texture combinations in which there is a gradual change in shape as well as a marked change in size of foliage. Of course, all of these shrubs thrive under the some general cultural conditions. In both cases you start out with a small quantity of your largest texture and end up with a large quantity of your finest texture. In the first instance, when the decrease in leaf size is more rapid and there are fewer steps in the transition, there should be a greater quantity increase with each step. When there are more steppings, as in the second example, the quantity of each step would not increase so rapidly, the net result showing about the same large amount of heather in either case.

The proportionate increase is not something rigid and inflexible. You don't simply multiply the number of shrubs. You have to take into account the size of each kind of shrub. For example, pernettya grows to three or four times the size of the winter flowering heather, *Erica carnea.* So one shrub might present three times as much foliage as another. Also one shrub often covers the base of another. You plan the increase so that there is a rhythmic increase in the amount of foliage which shows in the finished planting. For instance, you might start with a hybrid rhododendron, such as Pink Pearl, a tall leggy variety, and group from three to five shrubs of Oregon grape around it to clothe its base. Then arrange from three to five plants of *Pieris japonica,* on either side, which gives you from eight to ten plants of *Pieris.* Next, on either side beyond the *Pieris* group arrange anywhere from five to nine plants of evergreen huckleberry. Include several groups of three to five pernettya. Note that because they spread around you don't use many more plants of pernettya than evergreen huckleberry. As to the heather, you might use as many as one hundred plants, depending on the variety. This is how heather should be used—in a related mass instead of a few plants scattered around. (See figure 30.)

This discussion of closely knit sequences brings up a point about

27

A trio of broad-leaved evergreens in perfect sequence of foliage size grouped on the shady side of the house. The pattern of the *Aucuba japonica* at the left is picked up in the smaller foliage of the *Pieris japonica* (center) and carried over into the dainty sprays of *Azara microphylla.*

28

Sequence of broad-leaved evergreen foliage from large to small. Left to right: *Camellia japonica, Raphiolepis ovata, Mahonia aquifolium, Rhododendron Británnia,* Japanese pine. Heather in foreground.

Japanese table pine in center of picture has strength and character. Drifted up against the base is the handsome *Viburnum davidi*. Next to it *Arctostaphylos intermedia* provides a rapid step down in foliage size. Then the step to heather is equally rapid. This is a rhythmic sequence and therefore pleasing. Although the portion of the garden in this picture does not show it, there actually is a corresponding increase in quantity of smaller foliages as they step down, more of the *Arctostaphylos* than the *Viburnum* and much more of the heather than the *Arctostaphylos*.

Large sweeps of fine-foliaged texture punctuated by small areas of more vigorous texture. In foreground kinnikinnik with salal and Oregon grape poking through. Behind it heather (*Erica carnea Springwood white*). *Rhododendron augustini* blooming in center foreground.

A close sequence of medium-sized broad-leaved evergreen foliages. Right to left: *Aucuba japonica, Sarcococca saligna,* unclipped boxwood (*Buxus sempervirens*), and *Daphne odora.* Evergreen vine—*Akebia quinata.*

which there is justifiable controversy. The question is, when does a planting become too crowded? Some people feel that a planting is crowded if each plant does not stand out individually with plenty of light and air around it. But if you are planning drifts of sequences of broad-leaved evergreen foliage, the shrubs need to have their branches interlaced so that their foliage is woven into a tapestry-like design. In order to make an intelligent decision on this point, you need to be aware of the following points:

1. The ultimate height and spread of a plant
2. Its rate of growth
3. How long you are willing to wait for a mature effect
4. How much you accept the concept that interwoven foliage is not necessarily crowded

Many people of good taste feel that they are not fond of rhododendron foliage. They so often have seen unrelieved masses of it and disliked it, not realizing that their dislike probably was due to too great a quantity of large-sized foliage having been used instead of a well-related sequence. Long driveways banked with rows of massive rhododendrons may be very spectacular in bloom, but in terms of foliage texture they are hopelessly overpowering and monotonous.

A predominance of coarse-textured shrubs in a small-scaled garden dwarfs the whole area. You can imagine the effect in a small room if you were to use wallpaper with a pattern of huge roses two feet wide and chintz, on the same colossal scale, covering the furniture. The room would seem much smaller than its actual size, and you would feel dwarfed on entering it. Well, it is the same in a small garden. If you want it to appear larger than it really is, instead of smaller, you will work out your design in medium- to fine-foliaged textures. (See figure 31.)

When you are consciously using broad-leaved evergreen foliage for an effective pattern and texture, the natural foliage texture must be preserved. Therefore, never clip your shrubs. If any pruning is done, it must be done in such a way as to preserve and accentuate the plant's natural habit of growth. But what, you may say, is to be done if a plant is outgrowing its position? Isn't pruning the remedy, or rather clipping? Certainly not. One of the things about using plants as design materials is that instead of trying to subordinate them to your will, you must learn their natural habit of growth and their ultimate size. There are always shrubs to fit a given position.

Well-chosen broad-leaved evergreen shrubs, properly related to one another in foliage pattern and texture, provide immeasurable satisfaction.

deciduous shrubs and vines

9

DECIDUOUS shrubs often make a spectacular splash of color when they are in bloom—so much so that they are popularly known as "flowering shrubs." Their flowers—together with their constantly changing foliage color, from tender green in early spring through the various deeper greens in summer to yellow, bronze, orange, and scarlet in the fall—endear them to the gardener. However, their leafless branches in winter contribute much less to a permanently pictorial effect than the broad-leaved evergreens.

The colder the climate, the greater the proportion of deciduous shrubs in the natural vegetation and the smaller the proportion of broad-leaved evergreens. Some shrubs that are semi-evergreen in warmer regions are deciduous in colder ones. Few broad-leaved evergreens are hardy in the coldest climates. So the deciduous shrubs have to replace the broad-leaved evergreens as the principal items of shrub structure in the design of the cold climate garden. As is so often the case, nature compensates for this absence of broad-leaved evergreens. In regions where deciduous shrubs normally predominate, there is always some snow in winter, and this mantle of snow adds more beauty to the branches of the deciduous shrubs than it does to the broad-leaved evergreens.

Deciduous shrubs are often faster growing and thus less expensive than broad-leaved evergreens. So there is a tendency to use them for permanent structure planting even when numerous broad-leaved evergreens are available and should be given preference.

The soft foliage of deciduous shrubs makes a perfect background for herbaceous plants, while the glossy leathery leaves of the broad-leaved evergreens tend to pull away visually. Whenever broad-leaved evergreens can be used to give a permanent structure, deciduous shrubs should be used to fill in the sequence between fine-foliaged broad-leaved evergreens and the weak structural effect of herbaceous plants. The soft matte surface of deciduous leaves is essential in making the transition between herbaceous plants and the strong pattern and texture of broad-leaved evergreens. A comparatively large-leaved deciduous shrub is weaker and softer in effect than a broad-leaved evergreen with quite small leaves. The size of leaf of a broad-leaved evergreen is a determining design factor. But this is not equally true of deciduous shrub foliage. Therefore, it is effective to combine a large-leaved deciduous shrub with a broad-leaved evergreen that has leaves of much smaller size, provided there is a good relationship in foliage color and in the over-all effects produced by their habit of growth. For example, *Spirea thunbergi* blends pleasingly with *Berberis stenophylla gracilis* because they both have a somewhat arching habit of growth. Similarly *Azalea mollis* will relate well with evergreen huckleberry (*Vaccinium ovatum*) or the Japanese black-berried holly (*Ilex crenata*), because they all have a rather upright habit.

There are two basic ways of using deciduous shrub foliage color as a background for flowers. In summer the various greens provide a pleasant *cool color* foil for the masses of *warm flower colors* of the perennials. Reddish bronze and reddish purple foliages, such as the red-leaved Japanese barberry *(Berberis thunbergi atropurpurea),* Japanese purple-leaved plum (*Prunus pissardi*), and purple-leaved peach, may be used when desirable for contrast or sequence. In the fall you can work out thrilling sequences of *warm foliage color,* ranging from pure yellow through orange and bronze to scarlet and crimson and purple. Display *cool flower colors* against this warm background—for example, asters (Michaelmas daisies), which bloom prolifically at this season. Remember to observe naturalistic character in planning a sequence of foliage colors with deciduous shrubs.

Few deciduous shrubs have the distinctive branching pattern of deciduous trees. But since you must look at their bare branches for several months of the year, their pattern of lines does become a design factor. The densely twiggy, arching branches of most spireas do not combine effectively with the more heavily etched upshooting line of most deciduous azaleas, such as *Azalea mollis, A. pontica,* and *A. occidentalis.* A few deciduous shrubs have such a striking line pattern that

Plan 1

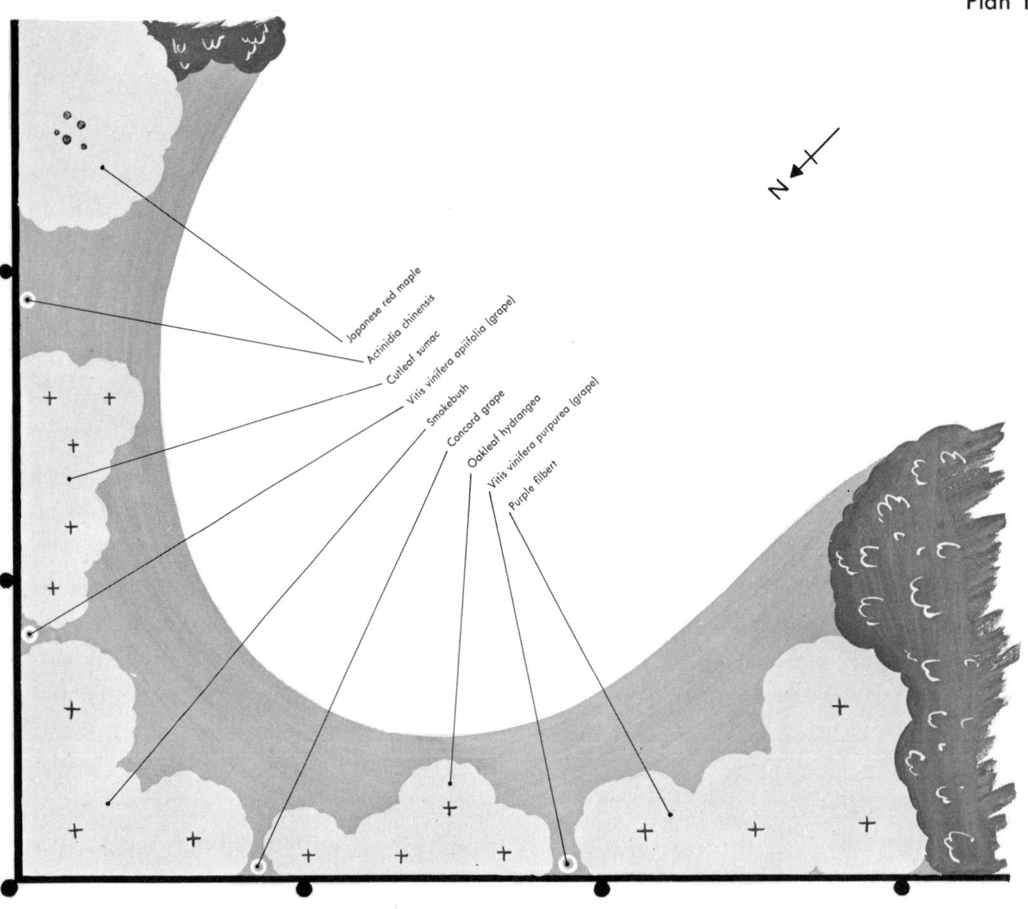

Fence: vertical rough-sawn boards, stained soft gray-green, 6 to 8 feet high.

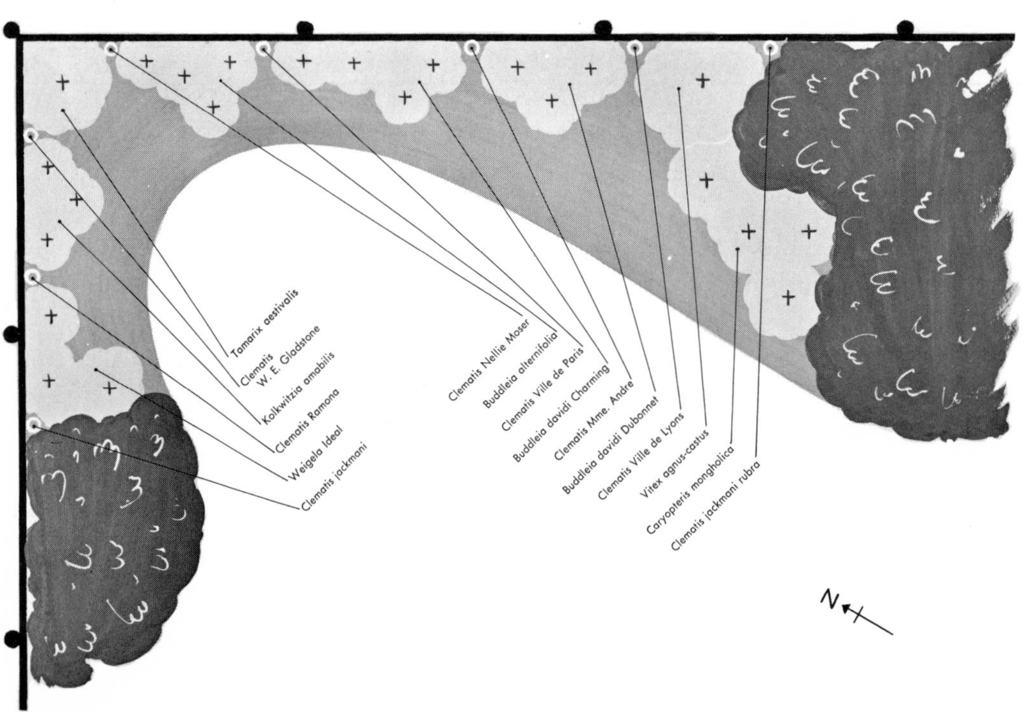

Plan 2

Plan 1 shows shrubs for a sunny corner. They are arranged to give a spectacular sequence of fall foliage color and a more subtle sequence of summer foliage color. The lightest fall color will occur at the deepest point of the incurve, with richer and stronger color building toward the outcurves. The color ranges from the deep red of the maple through the orange-red of the sumac to the yellow of the smokebush; then a similar sequence from the yellow of the smokebush to the red-orange of the hydrangea to the dark crimson of the filbert. The effect of these shrubs is supplemented by the vines planted to softly drape the fence. This background would blend pleasingly with the slightly gray-green foliage of chrysanthemums and the gray-foliaged hybrid aster (Michaelmas daisy) of the *novae-angliae* type, setting off their flowers to excellent advantage. The chrysanthemums should be yellow and bronze shades, the aster blue-lavender and purple in related sequences of color value and hue.

Plan 2 is a sunny corner grouping of shrubs chosen for their flowers rather than their fall colors. They range from the soft, fluffy pink spikes of the *Tamarix* in the corner to the crimson of the *Weigela Ideal* at one outcurve and the purple of the *Caryopteris* at the other outcurve. They are unified as a group by having variations of gray-green foliage. Their flowers are supplemented by a variety of summer flowering clematis, ranging in color from pink and lavender to crimson purple. These shrubs provide an attractive display of summer bloom in a pink to purple sequence. Also their gray foliage would be an excellent foil for a planting of chrysanthemums ranging from pink to crimson and gray-foliaged Michaelmas daisies ranging from lavender to purple, thus repeating the rhythmic sequence from paler colors in the incurve to darker colors at the outcurves.

Plan 3

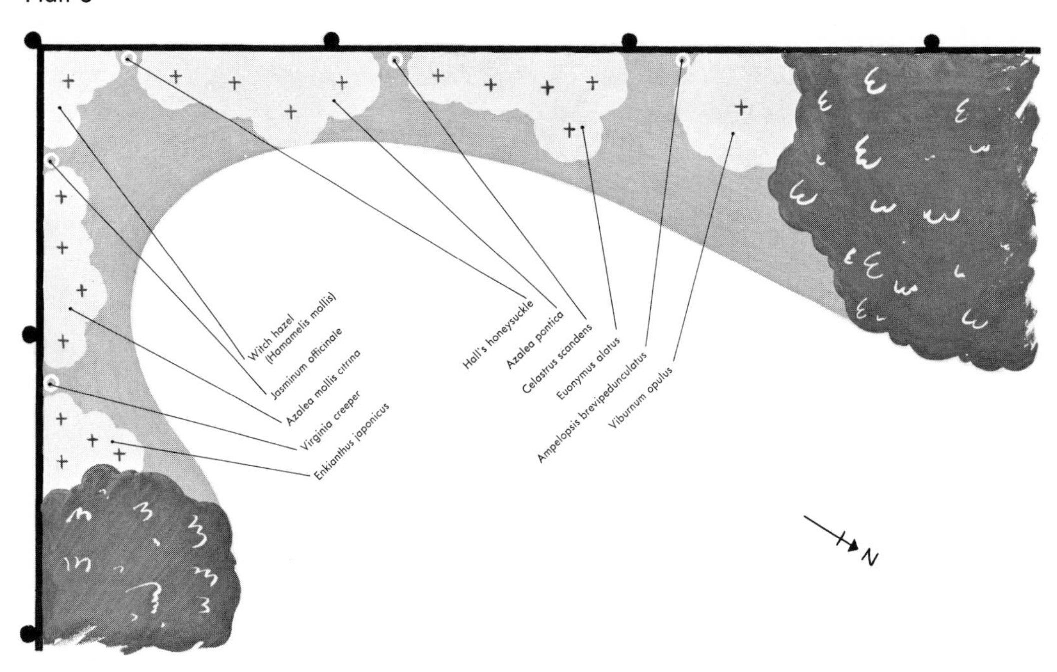

Fence: natural wood, weathered, 8 to 10 feet high.

Plan 3 is an example of choice spring flowering shrubs which like a moderate amount of moisture and partial shade. They are planted where they will get those conditions—on the north side of a high fence—and are arranged with direct reference to the color which their foliage takes on in the fall. Deep in the corner the winter-flowering witch hazel turns a clear light yellow. The azalea groupings on either side of it take on rich orange-bronze tones, while at one end of the grouping is the blood-red Japanese enkianthus and at the other the crimson snowball (*Viburnum opulus*). Herbaceous plants which like similar cultural conditions should be arranged in front of this shrub grouping. One of the most effective types of plants to feature in this case would be the lush green-foliaged dwarf and intermediate *Aster dumosus* hybrids (six to eighteen inches high), such as *Victor, Marjorie,* and *Blue Bouquet.* The flowers should be arranged with the whites, creams, and pale lavenders set back in the corner against the light yellow witch hazel foliage. The colors should become stronger as you build out to the outcurve in each direction. If you prefer, you could feature a herbaceous planting that would flower in spring and harmonize with the azaleas in bloom. For example, it would be a perfect spot to use primroses and polyanthus in a white, cream, yellow, orange, and bronze sequence with accents of forget-me-nots and scillas.

they could almost be considered to have the character and accentuation of deciduous trees. Sometimes they are grown as small trees—for example, the star magnolia (*Magnolia stellata*), the witch hazel (*Hamamelis mollis*), and the sumacs. Generally speaking, the densely twiggy shrubs are better used for massing while those with distinctive lines are better as individual specimens.

The intelligent pruning of deciduous shrubs to remove spent flowering wood is very important. It maintains their natural branching pattern. The all too common practice of clipping ruins their beauty by creating a congested mass of stubs. This ugliness is partially concealed in summer in a kind mantle of foliage, but it is painfully apparent in winter. A clipped deciduous shrub looks even worse in the winter than a clipped evergreen one.

Twiggy deciduous shrubs banked in front of coniferous evergreen foliage give an effect of confused line patterns that is not pleasing. So, in regions too cold for any broad-leaved evergreens, it is usually best to place conifers in free-standing groups by themselves. However, a coniferous evergreen tree that is bare of branches to a considerable height might have deciduous shrubs grouped at its base. In this case the pattern of branches would not be showing against the coniferous foliage. A blended mass of twiggy deciduous shrubs grouped at the base of a deciduous tree should form the main planting structure. This treatment is desirable only in the coldest climates where no broad-leaved evergreens are available.

vines

Deciduous vines have much the same function as deciduous shrubs. Evergreen vines are much the same in design effect as broad-leaved evergreen shrubs. In all but the very warmest sections the number of broad-leaved evergreen vines is small, the best known being the English ivy.

The primary use of deciduous vines is to give softening foliage and added interest in flower or foliage color. They fit into the garden design in any of the following ways:

1. To decorate a panel of wall or fence and make a tracery or line pattern against it. Such a panel with a properly trained vine can have all the grace, simplicity, and beauty of a Chinese wood block print. (See figure 32.)

2. To shade a porch, patio, or paved area. A deciduous vine provides shade in summer and also lets in plenty of light in the winter when the leaves are gone. This treatment does not call for any strong sense of design. It is simply a matter of distributing the main branches of the vine evenly over an area to provide a canopy of foliage that is not allowed to degenerate into an untidy tangle.
3. To give privacy when trained on an open fence or lattice, thus forming a protective screen of foliage. They can also be used to cover unattractive fences, transforming them into a pleasing background. A solid sheet of foliage can be obtained when the strength of the fence is sufficient to stand the weight of the vine. Evergreen vines are preferable for heavy, year-around screening. Since a dense mass of foliage is desirable, you can plant vines comparatively close together. Keep in mind that a screening plant becomes a background. Also remember to use a fine-textured rather than a coarse-textured foliage so that the background itself does not become too obtrusive.
4. To change the lines of a building and hide architectural faults, or to correct proportion in the division of space. This must be done with care and restraint.
5. To soften or completely change the texture of unattractive brick or concrete buildings—the use of Boston ivy on brick, for example. This use has the additional advantage of keeping a building cooler in hot weather.
6. To give added interest to large trees. Watch, in this case, that the vine selected is not such a strong one that it chokes the tree. Twining vines such as wisteria, small-flowered clematis, and fleece vine (*Polygonum baldschuanicum*) can be trained up into the top of a large mature tree, on a strong cord, and then allowed to ramble in the top of the tree. Don't let the vine twine its way up the trunk; rather lead it well into the head of the tree, keeping the growth of the vine free of laterals until it gets up above the main branches. Similarly smaller vines may be used on very large and vigorous shrubs. For example, an extremely interesting combination is the common snowball (*Viburnum opulus*), with its deep crimson tones in autumn contrasted with the bright blue berries of the ornamental grape (*Ampelopsis brevipedunculata*) rambling up through it.

Wisteria is especially attractive when trained in long, horizontal lines, widely spaced.

7. To supplement and fill in bare spots in the herbaceous border. Vines such as the late-blooming, large-flowered clematis may be planted behind clumps of perennials such as delphiniums. They can be trained up on stakes to cascade down over the foliage after the delphiniums are through blooming.

If vines are to have any design value, they must be properly trained. Their natural tendency is to run as rapidly as possible to the top of a supporting structure and make a great tangle of growth. To prevent this, start early by training a number of main stems horizontally to cover the desired space.

The training of vines partly depends on the nature of their growth. There are five main types:

1. The clinging, self-supporting vines such as Boston ivy, English ivy, and climbing hydrangea, which cling to brick, stone, or concrete and never need to be tied up or supported. They require considerable pruning when young in order to get shoots started in the right directions. Such vines can be destructive to wooden walls, especially shingle or clapboard.
2. The twining vines, like honeysuckle or wisteria, which wrap their stems in a spiral, or else, like clematis, hang on to a support by means of twining leaf stems. An open lattice work, or a structure made by stringing stout copper wires between heavy hooks in vertical or horizontal lines, or squares, provides effective methods for training.
3. A few vines, such as *Jasminum nudiflorum,* which like to remain prostate or trail on the ground. If allowed to trail down, they form a cascading curtain.
4. Climbing roses which send out long arching or trailing shoots ideal for training on wall, trellis, or pergola.
5. Climbing shrubs, such as the various species and varieties of pyracantha, escallonia, and euonymus, which may be grown as free-standing shrubs, but which are often more effective when trained flat against a wall. In all cases, direct all the energies of the shrub toward forming a good basic structure and do not restrict the growth to an area too small for it.

10 naturalistic character

SOME gardens have a right look—a oneness of design combined with enough variety to give the feeling that all the plants inevitably belong together. Never forget that every plant has a personality. Plants are like people. You want to bring together the plants which have something to say to each other. The secret lies in ecology—the study of the relationship of plants to their environment. For doesn't nature distribute plant life in such a way that the plants grow where they are best fitted to grow? However, you do not attempt to imitate nature in following the leadings of naturalistic character. You apply the principles of naturalistic character to a consciously man-made relationship. A strictly naturalistic garden is one in which a certain ecological grouping native to one particular area is reproduced. A well-designed informal garden often includes plants from many different parts of the world, but groups together those that like similar climatic and cultural conditions. This is no slavish imitation of nature. It is intelligent adaptation and interpretation. The best garden is not one in which you cannot tell where nature ends and man begins! It is one in which man's work, though apparent, does not violate naturalistic principles but is understandingly and consciously designed to be a work of art.

There is a simple key for recognizing what environment—sun or shade, moisture or drought—any given plant needs and which plants belong together. It is color of foliage. There is an inseparable relation between the culture of the plants and the color of their foliage. If you group together plants that like the same cultural conditions, you will not go very far wrong in the combination of their foliage colors. By putting shade-loving plants in the shade, sun-loving plants in the sun, and grouping together plants which like the same amount of moisture, you will find an underlying relationship in their foliage colors.

Think of the foliage colors that you see when you take a trip through a desert—mostly gray-green. The woolly gray-green foliages are characteristic of plants which grow in dry, sun-drenched areas. Plants that grow in ample moisture on the edges of streams or ponds have lush yellow-green foliage. You would never think of planting a cactus in a bog nor attempt to grow a bog iris in a desert. On the other hand, you may have trouble in placing plants that don't represent such extremes. Between these two extremes lies a wide range of leaf colors, varying with the gradual increase in the amount of moisture from woolly gray-green of the desert into a deep, dull, almost black green, from there into bronze-greens and deep green with bronzy new growth, then into the rich green greens, and finally into the yellow greens of waterside. It requires insight into a plant's requirements to know where it should fit into the garden picture.

You will agree that the color of the foliage in most gardens predominates over the color of the flowers, forming the background or foil. Too often gardeners think of foliage as just being "green." When you start to look around and realize how many different greens there are, you will find a whole new, fascinating world of beauty and adventure. It so happens that greens constitute our widest range of color perception. If you become "green conscious," you will find that the amount of subtle variation within the range of this one hue is almost unbelievable. And if you sincerely want to achieve a completely harmonious garden, you will train your eye to distinguish the many varieties in foliage green.

The relationship between foliage color and flower color is extremely interesting. When considering color schemes for the garden, do you immediately think about the color of the flowers? The first fundamental of a garden color scheme is the color of the foliage. If you start with the color of the foliage, you will have laid the foundation for a more satisfying result when the garden is in bloom as well as for a more pleasing effect when it is not in bloom.

Plants that grow in full sun usually have brilliantly hued flowers, and often these flowers are prolifically produced. Shade-loving or woodland plants, and plants native to climates where the sunlight is never intense for long periods of time, do not make such a spectacular profusion of color and have a small proportion of flowers to foliage. Again this points to a fundamental truth about color schemes in the garden that will save you many heartaches. It is not practical to try to get masses of color in the shade, so don't attempt it. On the other hand, you can work out the loveliest symphony of greens from cool and pale to deep, sparkling emerald, with just a delicate touch of white or cream or soft yellow flowers and the occasional sparse accent of scarlet berry.

Magenta and magenta purple are the strongly predominating hues of desert flowers. One reason that magenta is an unpleasant color in our watered gardens is that it has been separated from its essential foil of gray-green foliage and the grays and browns of desert rocks and sand and placed in jarring juxtaposition with the yellow-greens of lawns and watered garden plantings. You may have been conscious of disliking magenta in the garden. Now you can see why. You will also see how important it is not to mix the dry gray-greens in between the lush yellow-greens. In other words, do not combine gray-green foliage with yellow-green foliage any more than you would use magenta flowers with yellow-green foliage. They are equally inharmonious. However, it takes a more discerning eye to detect the discordant note in the combinations of green than to recognize the jarring effect of misplaced magenta.

You can design a graduated sequence of foliage color, changing with the variation in conditions from dry to moist or from sun to shade. These sequences of foliage color are especially noticeable in broad-leaved evergreen shrubs. Many of them like hot, dry conditions and have unmistakably woolly or glaucous gray-green foliage. Some examples are:

Arctostaphylos columbiana and related species (manzanita)
Cistus albidus, crispus, villosus, and hybrids (rock rose)
Cotoneaster francheti, harroviana, parnayi
Garrya elliptica (tassel bush)
Hypericum species and hybrids (St. John's wort)
Lavandula spica (lavender)
Rosmarinus (rosemary)
Veronica traversi, glauca

Another group which also requires hot, dry conditions in full sun—a group which has glossy yellow-green foliage and in many cases is noticeably aromatic—includes:

33

A lush waterside planting. At right strong reedy foliage of Japanese bog iris (*I. kaempferi*). Bright yellow flowers of globe flower (*Trollius*) harmonize with lush yellow green of all waterside foliages. Bamboo in background (right) is also a moisture lover as is Portugal laurel (left). Although this pool is man made, it is so constructed that it appears completely natural, being surrounded by a margin of marshy soil in which genuine bog plants thrive.

Ceanothus thyrsiflorus vars. and hybrids (California wild lilac)
Choisya ternata (Mexican orange)
Escallonia macrantha, rubra, and hybrids
Euonymus japonicus
Myrtus communis (Greek myrtle)
Veronica buxifolia

It is usually better not to combine these with the very gray-green foliages. Instead use them in a separate sequence of foliage color, working from yellow-green into the bronze or deep greens, then in a gradual transition into a lusher type of foliage. Consequently if you have a small area that is hot and dry you would use either the gray-green or the yellow-green foliages, but not both.

There are a few plants which adapt themselves to a fairly wide range of cultural conditions, and their foliage varies with these conditions. For example, *Mahonia aquifolium* (Oregon grape), growing under full sun in hot, dry conditions, turns darker and more leathery so that it blends very pleasingly with the leathery dark greens of shrubs like the following:

Cistus laurifolius, ladaniferus, loreti (rock rose)
Cotoneaster microphylla
Elaeagnus pungens
Eriobotrya japonica (loquat)
Laurus nobilis (bay laurel)
Viburnum tinus (laurestinus)

Oregon grape also blends equally well with other broad-leaved evergreen shrubs that grow in moister or shadier conditions, as shown by its inclusion in several of the following lists. The majority of shrubs do not grow well under such a wide range of conditions and must be grouped only with shrubs that like the same conditions that they themselves require.

The shrubs in the next group represent the middle range between the two extremes of dry and moist. Consequently they are shrubs which adapt themselves particularly readily to average conditions in a watered garden, although they prefer full sun. They have deep to medium green lustrous foliage and usually have bronze or coppery new leaves. In some instances the bronze of the new foliage is such an intense color that it makes an effect even more spectacular than flowers. One of the most noteworthy of these is the new foliage of *Photinia glabra.*

Abelia grandiflora, schumanni
Arbutus unedo (strawberry bush)
Azalea ledifolia, macrantha
Camellia sasanqua vars.

34

Woodland ground cover in the rain forest of western Washington. Note the lush yet delicate character of this combination of foliages—a pattern of horizontal planes with each leaf competing for a maximum of filtered light. The predominating foliage is wood sorrel (*Oxalis*).

Crisp-textured pattern of woodland ground cover on Alaska coast, the equivalent of subalpine woodland in more southerly latitudes. These plants adapt themselves well to garden use. Note difference in character between this and facing illustration. Creeping dogwood, oak fern, and *Coptis* make up this foliage tapestry.

Cotoneaster henryana
Erica carnea vars., *vagans* vars., and hybrids (heather)
Ilex cornuta, opaca, pernyi (holly)
Mahonia aquifolium, nervosa (Oregon grape)
Osmanthus ilicifolius
Phillyrea decora
Pernettya mucronata vars.
Photinia serrulata, glabra
Pieris floribunda, formosa (Andromeda)
Pyracantha atalantioides, rogersiana, yunnanensis (fire thorn)
Raphiolepis indica rosea
Rhododendron (small-leaved species) *augustini, ciliatum, yunnanense*

The next list consists of shrubs which will grow in even lusher conditions but prefer partial shade and moderate moisture—shrubs which have medium-green foliage:

Berberis darwini, stenophylla and vars., *verruculosa*
Buxus microphylla, sempervirens and vars. (box)
Camellia japonica vars. and hybrids
Daphne odora
Gaultheria shallon (salal)
Ilex aquifolium, crenata (holly)
Kalmia latifolia (mountain laurel)
Leucothoe catesbaei
Vaccinium ovatum (evergreen huckleberry)
Ligustrum japonicum (*lucidum* of gardens), *henryi*
Mahonia aquifolium, beali (Oregon grape)
Nandina domestica (Chinese sacred bamboo)
Pieris japonica (Andromeda)
Prunus laurocerasus (English laurel)
Raphiolepis ovata (Yeddo hawthorne)
Rhododendron, mostly garden hybrids, and species of medium leaf size such as *decorum, discolor,* and *ponticum*
Viburnum rhytidophyllum

Shrubs which want deep shade with moderate moisture have even lusher green foliage. They include:

Ardisia japonica, crenulata
Aucuba japonica
Fatsia japonica
Gaultheria shallon (salal)
Hedera helix arborescens (ivy)
Mahonia beali, nervosa (Oregon grape)
Pachistima myrsinites (false box)
Pachysandra terminalis
Prunus lusitanica (Portugal laurel)
Rhododendron, largest leaf species such as *falconeri*
Sarcococca, all species and vars.
Skimmia, all species and vars.
Vaccinium ovatum (Evergreen huckleberry)

The great majority of conifers thrive under the average conditions of moisture provided by a watered garden in sun. There are a few, however, with gray-green foliage, such as western juniper (*Juniperus occidentalis*), a native of the eastern Oregon sagebrush country, and the somewhat similar Arizona cypress (*Cupressus arizonica*), with very gray-green foliage, which thrive only in hot, dry conditions.

An instance of foliage color which might appear to the unwary to be a contradiction is the soft bluish gray of certain juvenile forms of *Chamaecyparis* (Retinospora). The best known of these is *Chamaecyparis pisifera squarrosa,* which is the juvenile form of the Japanese Sawara cypress listed by nurseries as *Retinospora squarrosa* or *R. s. veitchi.* All such conifers with juvenile foliage do best when grown in light shade and ample moisture. If you attempt to grow them in full sun and under dry conditions, they will quickly get dull and dingy looking for the simple reason that they are not getting what they need. It is interesting to note how harmoniously they blend with the soft greens of the other shade-loving plants. This is another proof that an understanding of the cultural requirements of plants is a far better guide to satisfactory combinations than any set rule or formula for foliage color.

The same principles apply to the deciduous shrubs as to the broad-leaved evergreens. Those with drought-resistant, gray-green foliage include:

Buddleia (butterfly bush)
Caryopteris (blue spirea)
Elaeagnus angustifolia, argentea, umbellata
Hippophae (sea buckthorn)
Cytisus (broom)
Kolkwitzia (beauty bush)
Tamarix
Vitex

Those with deep green foliage and bronzy new growth liking full sun and moderately dry conditions include:

Azalea, species such as *kaempferi, mollis, pontica*
Prunus glandulosa (flowering almond)
Chaenomeles, all species and hybrids (flowering quince)
Punica granatum vars. (flowering pomegranate)
Viburnum burkwoodi, opulus (snowball)

Shrubs with medium green foliage growing in full sun and needing slightly more moisture include:

Azalea, species such as *occidentalis, schlippenbachi, vaseyi*

Rosa, species such as *hugonis, moyesi, rugosa*

Syringa vulgaris hybrids (lilac)

Hydrangea hortensis has lush green foliage, which indicates that it is happiest with a great deal of moisture.

Shrubs growing best in light, deciduous shade with moderate moisture include:

Forsythia, all species and hybrids (golden bell)

Kerria japonica

Philadelphus, all species and hybrids (mock orange)

Rhodotypos kerrioides (jet bead)

Spiraea, species such as *thunbergi, van houttei*

There are few if any deciduous flowering shrubs which grow well in deep shade.

As to herbaceous plants, the designer is only concerned with the plants that grow well under average garden conditions. Most of these are hybrids—man-made flowers without very strong naturalistic character. Consequently they will grow well together and, instead of having distinctly individual requirements, they are happy in a "mess of comfort in the garden." However, to use them the most effectively, group them as though they did have distinct cultural requirements and place together those with gray foliage (descended from ancestors which much preferred dry conditions). Similarly those with lusher green foliage should be combined even though they will all grow in the same herbaceous border with the same amount of moisture. The Michaelmas daisies are a good example of this sort of thing. There are some whose forebears grew in moist marshy ground, and they have lush green foliage. There are others whose ancestors came from dry cliffs and rock ledges, and they have gray-green foliage. Both races of hybrids will thrive under the same conditions in the garden, but it is much more effective to group the gray-foliaged ones with chrysanthemums, for example, and the green-foliaged ones with perennial phlox. Creating an illusion of naturalistic character by a sequence of foliage color will do wonders in building a basic color scheme for the perennial border.

Gray-foliaged herbaceous plants include:

Aster (Michaelmas daisy), gray-foliaged species and hybrids such as *frikarti, amellus,* and some of the *novae-angliae* hybrids

36

Naturalistic planting along a stream features the reedy foliage of the common daylily. Upstream is the bold foliage of skunk cabbage.

In a planted garden a lush effect is produced in partial shade with the foliages of *Funkia* (*Hosta*) and hybrid daylilies, with rhododendron foliage in the background.

37

A mossy woodland path winding through a hazel copse. Planting combines sword ferns, salal, trillium with the more cultivated touches of primroses and polyanthus. Foliage in lower right foreground is *Epimedium*, a useful woodland plant.

Chrysanthemum, garden hybrids
Iris (German), hybrid-bearded
Nepeta mussini
Santolina chamaecyparissus (lavender cotton)

Peonies and *Statice latifolia* are examples of herbaceous plants with bronzy new foliage and deep green mature foliage.

Herbaceous plants with medium green foliage include:

Delphinium
Helenium
Rudbeckia (goldenglow)

Herbaceous plants with lusher green foliage growing in light shade with moderate moisture include:

Aster (Michaelmas daisy), species and hybrids with deep green foliage, including most of the *novi-belgi* hybrids (prefer ample moisture in full sun)
Cimicifuga (bugbane)
Hemerocallis (daylily)
Phlox paniculata hybrids
Primula acaulis hybrids (primroses and polyanthus)

Those with deep green leaves growing in deep shade with moderate moisture include:

Epimedium
Ferns
Hosta (*funkia* or plantain lily)
Helleborus niger (Christmas rose)
Lily of the valley
Violets

herbaceous plants

11

HERBACEOUS plants are the flesh clothing the structure of the garden, giving softness and color. They may be annuals, biennials, or perennials, but in all cases they die down to the ground at the conclusion of their flowering season and do not form a permanent woody growth. In this sense they are not structural design materials.

Most of the mistakes that are made in using herbaceous plants in garden design stem from the unconscious attempt to use them as though they were structural materials. If you analyze the borders and herbaceous plantings that you have found pleasing, you will realize that they were supported by a strong structural background or enframement.

The background must be planned to support but not compete with the herbaceous planting. This does not mean that the background should be lacking in interest, but the interest which it provides must be subordinated and subtle, as well as carefully keyed to the floral display which it is meant to show off. Hedges, whether closely or loosely clipped, are often used as a garden boundary and background, but they are rapidly becoming less popular because of their high maintenance. Large-leaved trees or shrubs, such as English laurel, are particularly undesirable as background hedge material because of the coarse-textured effect they produce. A soft, fine-textured (small-leaved) hedge may make a satisfactory background for flowers, but some provision must be made to prevent the roots of the hedge from invading and robbing the richly prepared soil of the flower bed. The initial cost of a fence or wall is greater than that of planting a young hedge, but in the long run a fence costs no more and is virtually free of maintenance. Some walls and fences are planned to give considerable architectural interest. (See color illustration of tulips, page 127.) In many cases this is entirely desirable, but if you plan to use a fence or wall as a background for herbaceous planting be careful that it is not too "busy." The frequent architectural "busy-ness" of a house with its windows, doors, and other features is one reason why it is not satisfactory to use the wall of a house as a border background. When the border is in bloom, there is conflicting interest to distract the eye. When the border is not in bloom, there is an awkward gap, often an untidy one. A simple, unobtrusive, yet pleasing fence or wall is a good background, especially if you drape it gracefully with deciduous flowering vines such as clematis and honeysuckle and also plant drifts of deciduous shrubs in front of it. (See figure 39.) With this background and enframement, flowers are like jewels in an appropriate setting.

Herbaceous plants, as a whole, are attractive for a comparatively short time. Also most of them require much more care than trees and shrubs. A garden with nothing but herbaceous plants is bound to look unattractive for long periods unless the area is constantly groomed. Thus the combination of high maintenance, short-term effectiveness, and nonstructural growth is shunned by experienced gardeners. Usually they do not attempt gardens devoted exclusively to perennials. Exceptions occur in large estates in which individual segregated gardens are devoted to flower borders or one-flower gardens—for example, iris gardens, peony gardens, rose gardens. You don't have to look at these gardens except when they are at their prime.

What is the solution then? For perennials, annuals, and bulbs certainly do have an important place in the garden picture. The solution is to plan your garden so that it will be effective and satisfying *without any herbaceous plants.* Then add them for seasonal color. In this kind of planning you do not miss them when they are out of bloom. And you get the fullest pleasure when they are in bloom because they are effectively enframed by the permanent structure. (See drawings illustrating "bad, better, best.")

Keep your herbaceous planting simple. You may have read dissertations on how to have masses of bloom all summer long. Such promises are like politicians' election speeches. They are seldom practical and present a false objective. The realistic approach is to take one limited area and feature in it plants which are at their peak of effectiveness at one season—in spring and early summer, for instance. Then use another area for plants which are at their height in midsummer, and another for those which bloom in the fall. This does not mean that each area will be completely flowerless when it is not in full bloom. There can be light touches of color at other times in the growing season. But if you try for a constant succession of bloom within one small space, you will find that you inevitably end up with a spotty effect. On the other hand, there are many useful tricks for successfully introducing extra color throughout the season. For example, interplant baby dahlias among peonies, planting them late enough in the season so that they come up through the peony foliage well after the peonies are through blooming. Taller dahlias can be interplanted through delphiniums toward the back of the border. Vines can be trained on stakes or on a fence at the back of the border and draped down over perennials that have begun to get untidy. The large-flowered, summer-flowering clematis is especially effective used this way.

Before you actually plan your flower planting, consider carefully just how much time you can give to it. For minimum care and maximum effect, use the following combination:

1. Mostly perennials which require infrequent divisions (for example, peonies, which go on developing from year to year).
2. A few perennials which require frequent dividing (every one or two years).
3. Still fewer annuals or bedding plants, such as petunias, geraniums, or snapdragons, which give color almost all summer long.
4. Bulbs interplanted with the more permanent perennials or among shrubs. Daffodils and some of the lilies may be naturalized and require practically no care at all. Garden tulips must be taken up and replanted almost every year to get the best results; so they do not belong in a minimum maintenance scheme.

Watch that you don't crowd too great a range of color or too many varieties of plants into the planting space.

The plans in this chapter show how herbaceous plants may be used in small gardens by setting them back in in-curves and enframing them with shrub groupings and vine-covered fences. All of the plants in their respective groupings like the same cultural conditions. They are all shade-loving in the spring border and sun-loving in the fall border.

TO BE EFFECTIVE
A FLOWER BORDER
MUST HAVE
A GOOD BACKGROUND

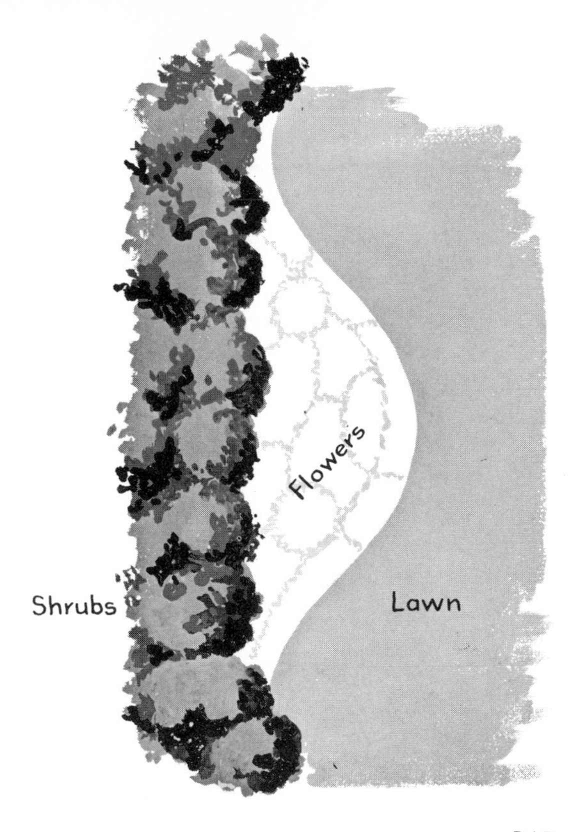

BAD

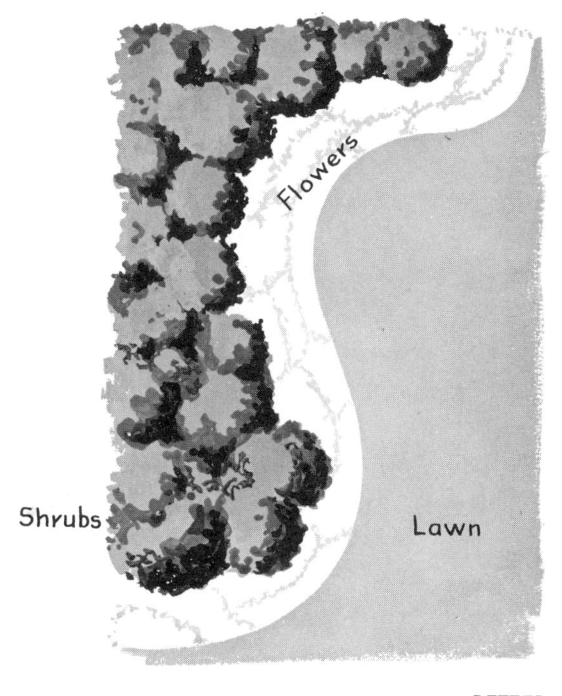

BETTER

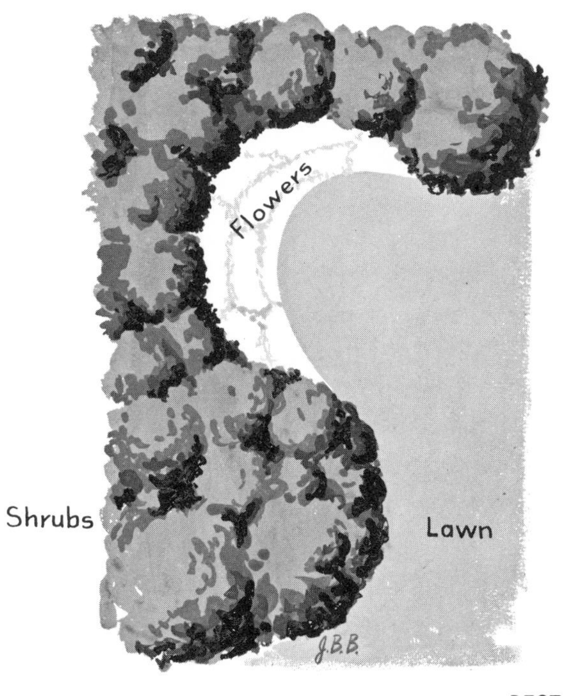

BEST

This brings about a unity of naturalistic character which is evidenced in a symphony of harmonious foliage color.

The spring border was designed to produce its *main effect* at the time daffodils are in bloom. However, it would be attractive all through the season because of long-lasting foliage effects, even though the touches of flower color are light. It would be possible to keep concentrated color all summer by taking the primroses out as soon as they are through blooming and planting them in a reserve area, replacing them with tuberous begonias in the same color range. But if you are not too "color hungry" you may prefer to forego this shuffling and have a quiet, cool green corner, with light touches of color from plantain lily or other later bloomers during the summer.

The fall border would be bare in the spring unless you chose to mass tulips in the spaces allotted to annuals (i. e., the petunias, snapdragons, and stocks). This is rightly called a fall border because the chrysanthemums and Michaelmas daisies which predominate in the perennial planting reach their climax in September and October and the annuals are still in full bloom at that time. But the annuals will have been making a very good showing all through the summer, backed by the harmonious foliage colors of the Michaelmas daisies and chrysanthemums before they come into bloom.

The spring border has low maintenance because so many of the perennials used can be left in one spot without dividing or replacing them for several years at a time. The primroses, however, should be divided and replanted immediately after flowering every other year or at the very least once in three years.

The fall border rewards you with heavier masses of color over a longer period but demands proportionately higher maintenance. The chrysanthemums and Michaelmas daisies should be divided and replanted every spring, and of course the annuals must be replaced each year. But even so, to make it simpler to care for them you will find it more practical to have all such plants grouped in *one* area than to scatter them around your garden helter-skelter.

The underlying theory of color schemes of both these borders is discussed in Chapter 15.

flower forms—spike and round-headed

Plan 6 shows a midsummer border with one solution of the problem of combining effectively the spike form of flowers like delphiniums with

39

An old-fashioned English herbaceous border backed with deciduous shrubs and vines. A simple fence and gateway covered with fleece vine (*Polygonum*) help give structure to the composition.

40

Brick paving and brick retaining walls form a solid structure pleasingly softened and draped with herbaceous plants.

the contrasting round-headed flower forms like peonies, Oriental poppies, and so forth. Grouping flower forms in a border is like grouping notes into musical ideas or themes and developing them into a symphony. The construction of the simplest symphony is relatively complex and yet every symphony conforms to the laws of harmony. Each individual composer may produce distinctly individual symphonies, but there are certain basic principles of construction which are evident in all. The same thing is true when grouping flowers in a border. You can get the best results only by understanding the underlying principles and all the different elements of the composition, just as the musician must do before he can compose good music.

The form of the flowers is one of the most important design elements to be considered. There are three main classifications: (1) the spike, (2) the round-headed form (either of individual flowers or clustered flower heads), and (3) the intermediate shape. Plan 6 shows a strong interplay of spike versus round-headed forms which, like counterpoint in music, helps to build the scene dramatically. The bold spikes of the delphiniums are echoed in the lupines, and later in the season snapdragons repeat this form. The lilacs in the background also carry their flowers in spikes. Round-headed forms here include peonies, Oriental poppies, and, later in the season, the geraniums and dahlias. The bearded iris is intermediate, although it is closer to round-headed than to spike form. The climbing roses on the fence add their quota of the round-headed form, and showing against the spikes of the delphinium as they do they further strengthen this study in contrasting form. The dahlias, geraniums, and snapdragons are sparsely planted among the groupings of perennials to give just a touch of color later in the season and to help hide untidy foliage as it dies down. Oriental poppies, especially, need this coverage because their foliage usually dies down completely by the middle of the summer.

This border plan shows what might be considered a maximum use of spike form. Beware of using the spike form too much or indiscriminately. Unless it is placed with care and understanding it will break up the composition. On the other hand, if you omit the spike form the composition will be in danger of lacking interest and accent. However, there is nothing difficult in this design problem. Once you have become thoroughly conscious that these two flower forms exist, you will enjoy combining them both in flower arrangements in the house and as growing plants in the garden. Wrong use of them springs mainly from

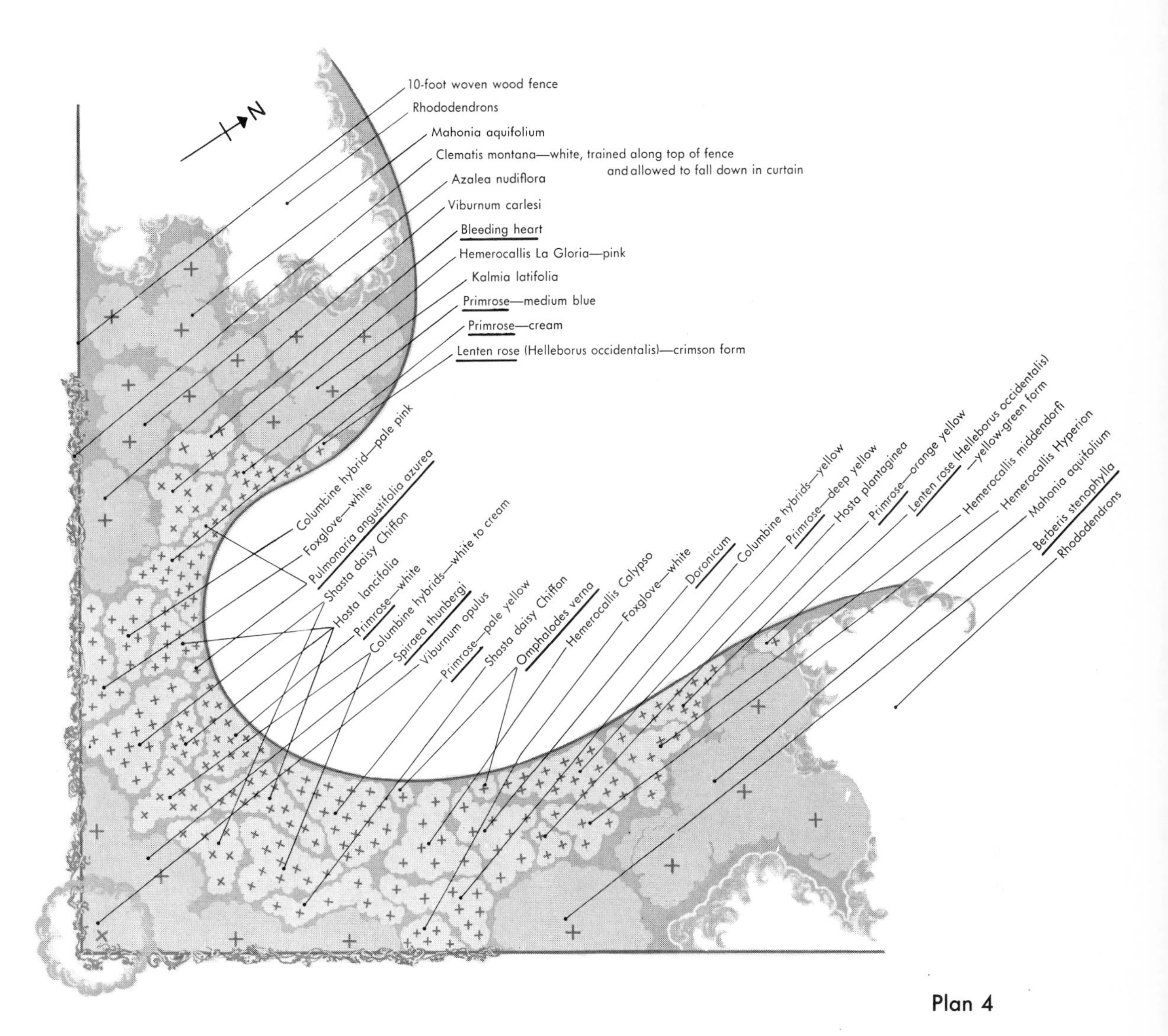

Plan 4

SPRING BORDER, PARTIAL SHADE

Underlined words indicate perennials and shrubs in bloom in early spring. These are followed by the rest of the shrubs in late spring and by the remainder of the perennials in summer. For bulb planting in this border see Plan 4a.

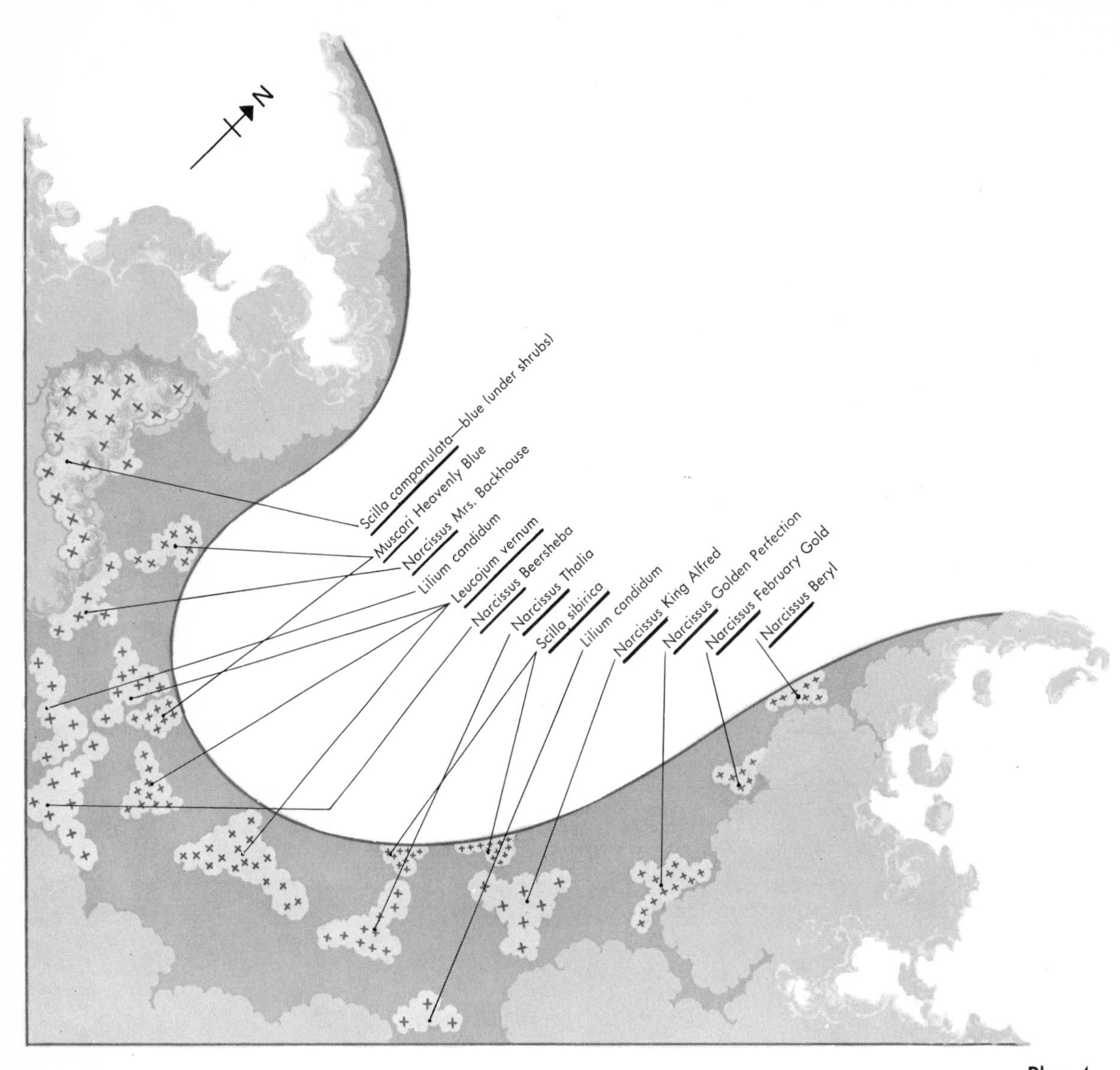

Plan 4a

SPRING BULB PLAN

This adds more spring color—that of bulbs—to the perennial border (Plan 4). It is made up as a separate plan to make both plans easier to read. To see how they dovetail, place a tracing of this bulb plan over the other one.

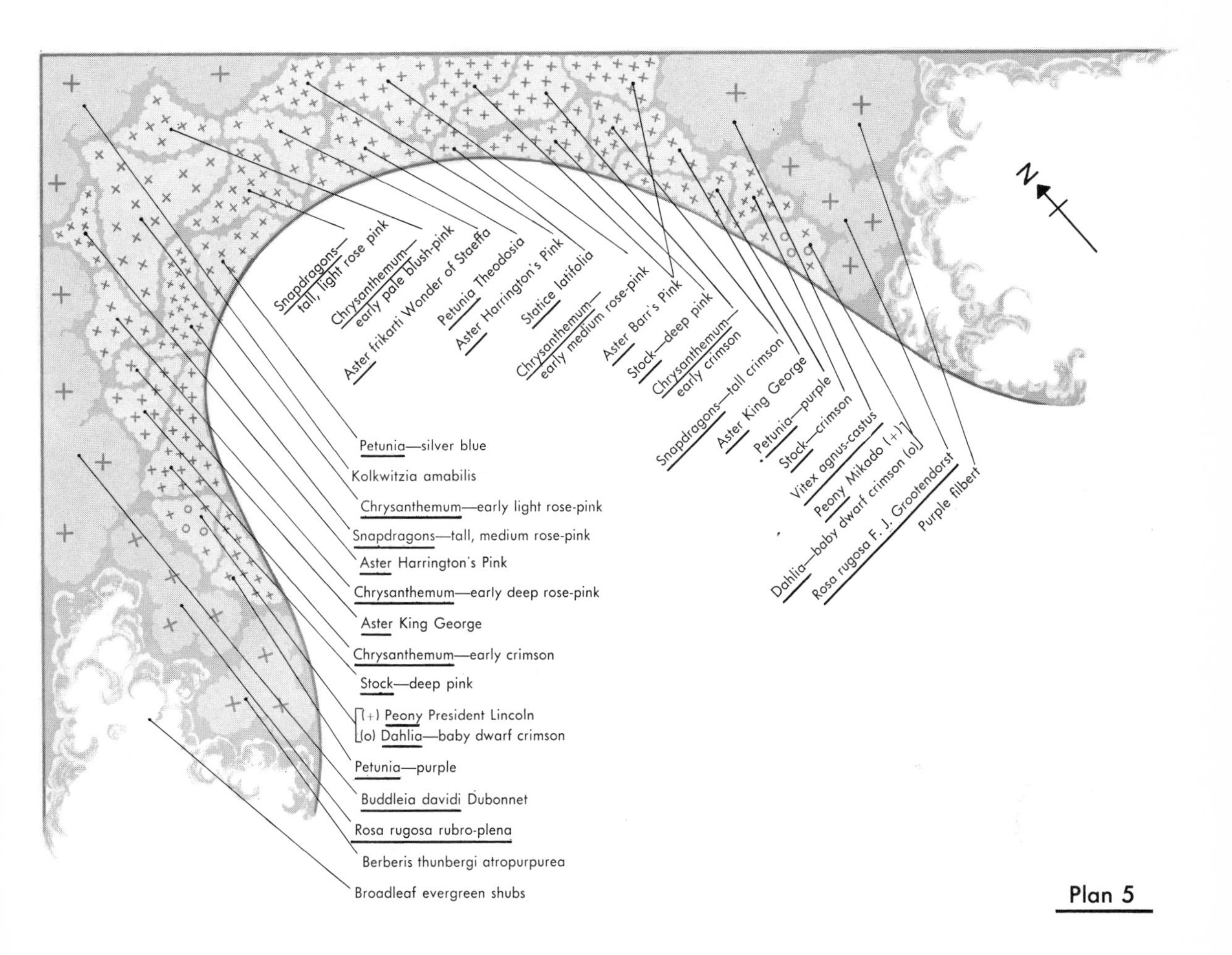

Plan 5

BORDER PLANTING
FOR MAXIMUM EFFECT IN EARLY FALL

Chrysanthemums and asters join annuals, dahlias, and a few late blooming shrubs for a fine show in early fall. Underlined plants are those blooming in September. The others give a touch of color before the annuals start to bloom.

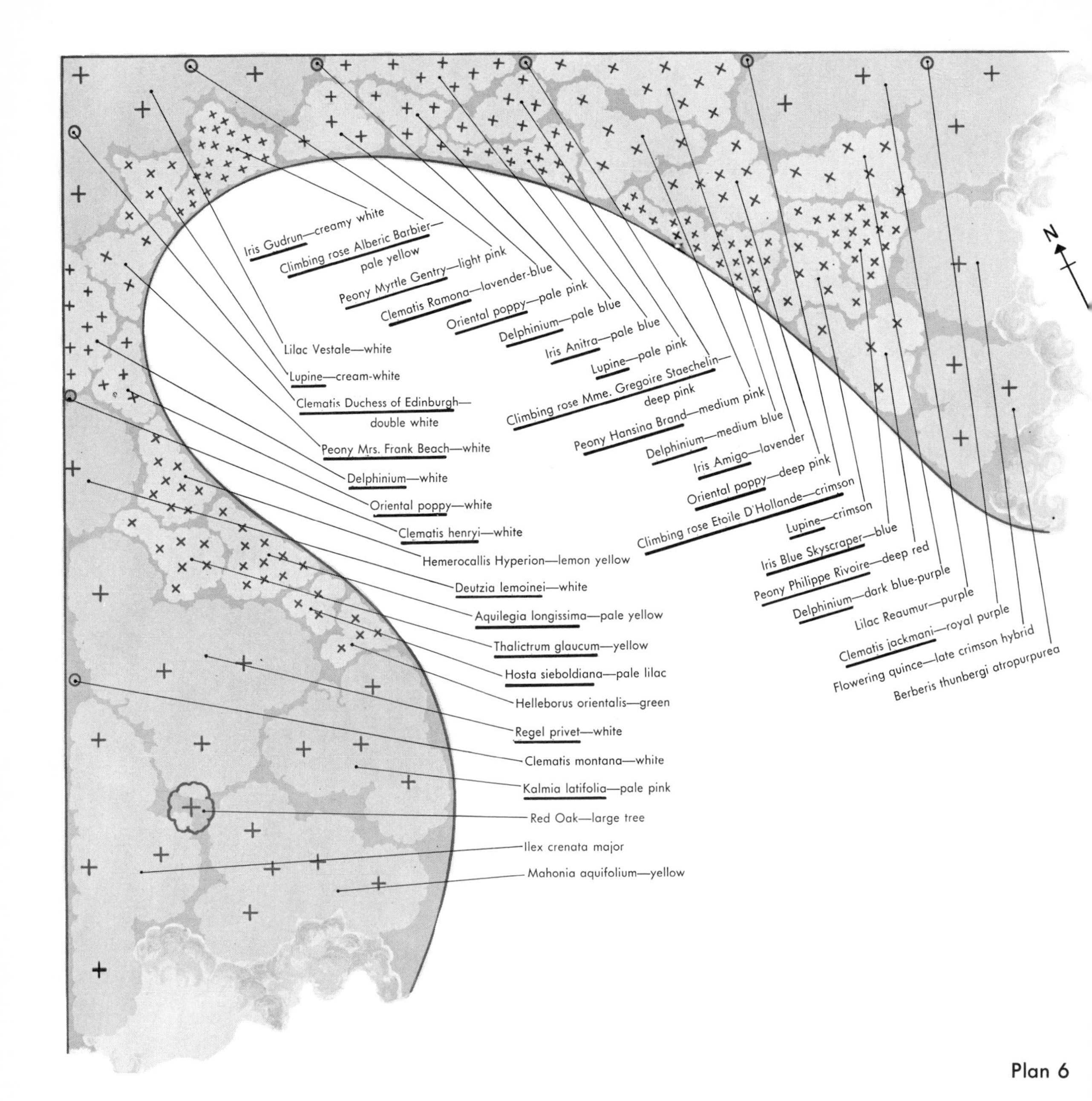

Plan 6

MIDSUMMER BORDER

This is the master plan for a midsummer border with an interplay of spike versus round flowers. Underlined names indicate the perennials, trees. shrubs, and vines in bloom.

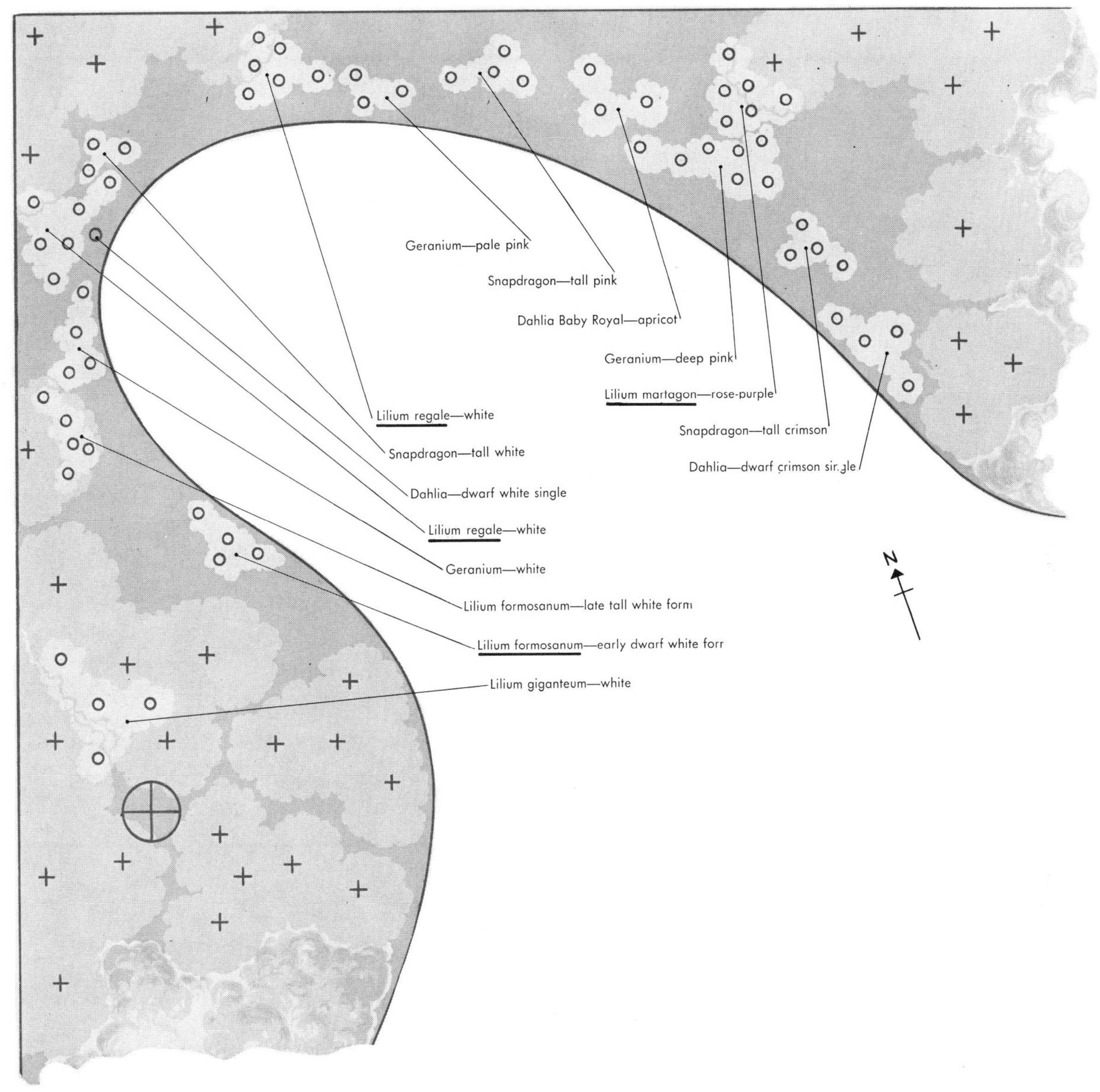

Plan 6a

MIDSUMMER BORDER (SUPPLEMENTARY PLAN)

This planting plan for bulbs, annuals, and bedding plants is made separately in order to simplify things for the planter. To see how the two plans dovetail, place a tracing of this plan over the master one.

a lack of awareness of what they do for a composition. Remember that the spike form usually becomes an accent, but avoid the indiscriminate scattering of accent points throughout the composition.

Establish the points of accentuation and then build around them a sequence or series of sizes of round-headed forms that are rhythmically related. In Plan 3 the Oriental poppies, the peonies, and the iris are related in scale, the individual flowers of each being fairly large. Yet there is a gradation of size. The hybrid peonies are the largest of the round-headed forms. The average Oriental poppy bloom will be a step smaller than the peonies, and the iris blooms in turn will be smaller than the Oriental poppies. You can readily see that if much smaller round-headed flowers had been introduced into this competition, they would have been out of scale with the existing sequence of large round-headed flowers. For example, small-scale flowers, like scabiosa and Iceland poppies, could not have held their own in this particularly large-scale dramatic grouping.

Foliage form, too, has a great deal to do with the effectiveness of the border and for a much longer period than merely when the border is at its peak of bloom. Strong reedy foliage, such as that of the iris, adds strength and snap to the composition. Whether the planting is in sun or shade, there is always some appropriate reedy foliage that may be used. The lush green of the *Hemerocallis Hyperion* is used to provide this foliage accent in the semishade area to the north of the oak tree. The glaucous green of the bearded iris belongs on the sunny side.

spacing

All problems in design involve problems in spacing. This design problem is more complex in grouping herbaceous plants because they have such different habits of growth and spread at varying rates. It takes special know-how to plan for and maintain good spacing from year to year. Even the original planting requires a special technique so that overcrowding or gaps are avoided. Such a technique achieves the easy grace of a community of plants comfortably adjusted to one another.

The first step in establishing a pleasing sense of space is to recognize that herbaceous plants, since they do not have a permanent structure and distinct individuality of form, should be used in groups or drifts rather than as individual specimens. Therefore, in planting a border the drift, and not the individual plant, becomes the *unit of planting*. The question of drifts is important in any garden planting, but it is especially important in grouping herbaceous plants, because it is the *shape of the group* which contributes most to the design. Woody plant material can stand out independently. For example, you might use a tree, such as an oak, maple, or cherry, free-standing in the middle of your lawn, and it could be effective in the design. But you would not think of putting a delphinium all by itself in the middle of your lawn. Perhaps that is an extreme example. But it indicates what we mean when we say that perennials must be used in groups or drifts of interesting shape in order to really count for something in the design, even when in bloom. To make the shape of the drift apparent, allow more space between drifts than between plants within any given drift. This gives form to the drift and eliminates an effect of overcrowding even though the plants may be fairly close within the drift. If there is sufficient space from one drift to another, your planting will not look congested.

Next consider the different rates of growth or spread of different types of plants. It is perhaps simplest to divide these into three groups, as follows.

Group 1. Plants which spread rapidly need frequent dividing and replanting, preferably every year or at least every other year:

Achillea (milfoil or yarrow)
Artemisia lactiflora (ghostplant or wormwood)
Aster (Michaelmas daisy including New England aster, *A. novae angliae,* and New York aster, *A. novi-belgi,* and their varieties, but not *Aster frikarti* and other *Aster amellus* hybrids that are less vigorous)
Boltonia (false chamomile)
Eupatorium
Helenium (sneezeweed or Helen's flower)
Helianthus (sunflower)
Lysimachia (loosestrife)
Physostegia (lion's-heart)
Primula hybrids (primroses and polyanthus) and the Asiatic species such as *P. japonica, sieboldi, pulverulenta, bulleyana,* etc.
Ranunculus (buttercup or crowfoot)
Rudbeckia, including coneflower and goldenglow
Solidago (goldenrod)

Group 2. Plants which spread more slowly than those in Group 1 are divided every four or five years:

Aconitum (monkshood)
Anchusa myosotidiflora (bugloss)
Anemone japonica (windflower)
Armeria (thrift or sea pink)
Artemesia Silver King
Astilbe (perennial spirea)
Bocconia (plume poppy)
Campanula persicifolia (bellflower)
Catananche (cupid's dart)
Centaurea macrocephala
Chrysanthemum maximum (shasta daisy)
Delphinium hybrids
Dianthus hybrids (pinks)
Doronicum (leopard's-bane)
Echinacea purpurea (coneflower)
Filipendula hexapetala (dropwort)
Gaillardia (blanket flower)
Geum (avens)
Heliopsis (perennial sunflower)
Hemerocallis (daylily)
Heuchera (coral bells)
Hosta (Funkia) (plantain lily)
Iris (bearded and beardless)
Linum (flax)
Lychnis (campion or catchfly)
Monarda (bee balm or bergamot)
Nepeta (catmint)
Omphalodes verna (navel wort)
Phlox hybrids
Polemonium (Jacob's ladder)
Potentilla (cinquefoil)
Pulmonaria (lungwort)
Pyrethrum roseum (painted daisy)
Stachys lanata (lamb's ears)
Stokesia (Stoke's aster)
Tradescantia (spiderwort)
Veronica (speedwell)
Viola (violas and violets)

Group 3. Plants which spread slowly or resent moving, and are best undisturbed for eight or ten years or more, should not be put too close together in the original planting:

Anchusa, other than *myosotidiflora* (bugloss)
Baptisia australis (wild indigo)
Bergenia (Megasea) cordifolia (big-leaf saxifrage)
Callirrhoe involucrata (poppy mallow)
Centranthus (valerian or garden heliotrope)
Clematis, bush types
Dicentra (bleeding heart)
Dictamnus (gas plant or fraxinella)
Echinops (globe thistle)
Eremurus (desert candle)
Eryngium (eryngo or sea holly)
Galega officinalis (goat's-rue)
Geranium grandiflorum (lilac geranium or cranesbill)
Gypsophila (baby's-breath)
Helleborus (hellebore)
Hibiscus moscheutos (common rose mallow)
Kniphofia (Tritoma) (torch lily or red hot poker)
Liatris (gay-feather)
Limonium latifolium (wideleaf sea lavender)
Lythrum (purple loosestrife)
Lupinus (lupin)
Mertensia (Virginia bluebells)
Oenothera (evening primrose)

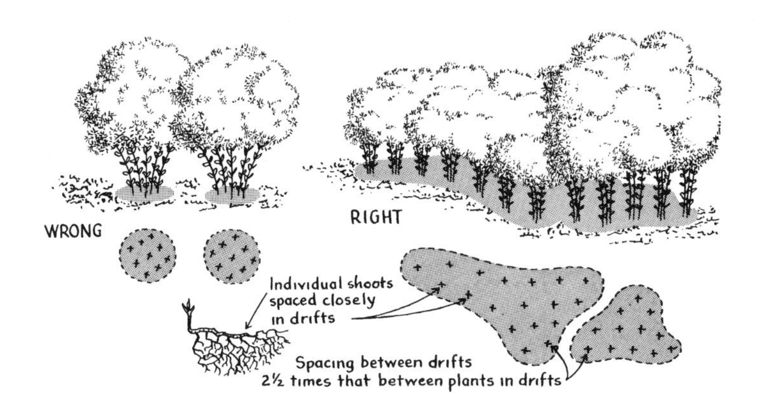

Group 1

Example: hardy aster (Michaelmas daisy). Transplant this every spring or every other spring, spacing 6 to 8 inches apart. Leave 15- to 20-inch space between drifts.

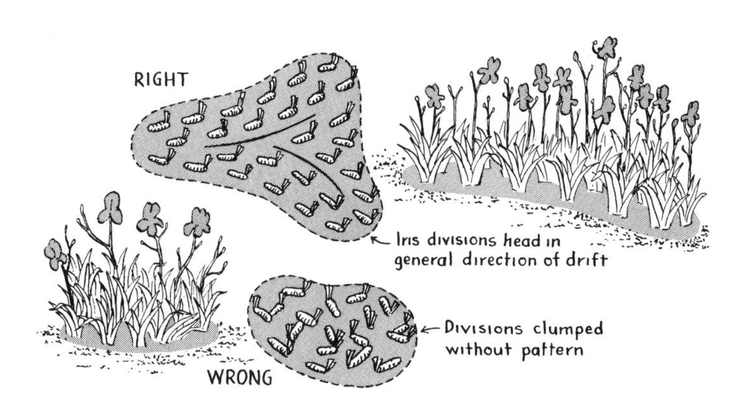

Group 2

Example: bearded iris. Transplant every four or five years, after blooming. Space divisions 12 to 18 inches apart. Special technique for iris: face all rhizomes in the same direction.

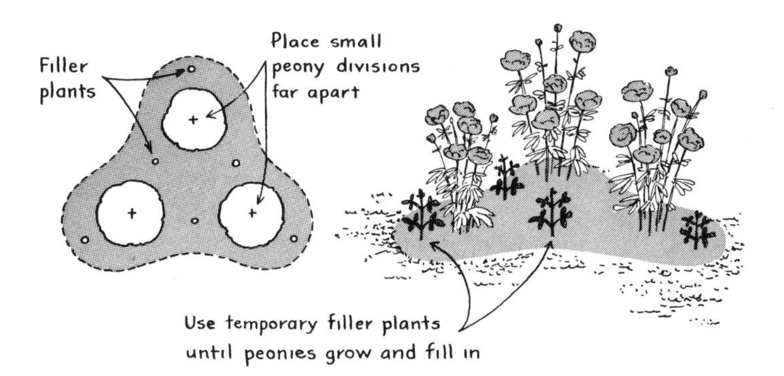

Group 3

Example: peony. Set the plants at least 3 feet apart. They can stay in place for years. Use fillers like Oriental poppies, tulips, and/or dahlias until peonies reach mature size.

Ophiopogon (lily turf)
Paeonia (peony)
Papaver orientale (Oriental poppy)
Perovskia (perowskia)
Polygonatum (Solomon's seal)
Sedum spectabile (showy stonecrop)
Sidalcea
Thalictrum (meadow rue)
Thermopsis caroliniana
Trollius (globe flower)

The first step in dealing with each of these groups is to decide upon, and to outline the size and shape of, the drift into which you intend to place the plants. Individual plants in Group 1 are divided into *single individual shoots* in the spring. These individual shoots are spaced from six to eight inches apart within the drift. (See Group 1 drawing.) Then each year these should be divided and replanted, getting rid of the surplus. If this is more work than you can manage, the plants will still be reasonably attractive if divided every other year. Don't let them go longer than that, however. Such fast-growing plants impoverish the ground, resulting in crowded stems and poor quality blooms. The replanting provides an opportunity to spade generous quantities of fertilizer into the ground.

Too often perennials in this class are grown in clumps or dense bunches of weak, spindly shoots instead of being planted out as described. This lumpiness and unattractive spacing is further accentuated by improper scaling. Usually a string is looped around each overgrown clump and the clump tied to a stake. Plants that are openly spaced within the drift usually develop strong enough individual stems to hold themselves up. This is especially true in the case of the best improved varieties of border perennials. But when necessary, the stalks should be individually staked and tied.

The spacing within the drifts for plants in Group 2 varies slightly with the individual plant. (See Group 2 drawing.) Some tend to degenerate over a period of years and others grow into a solid, crowded mass that will respond to dividing. Try to space them in such a way that they won't become too crowded until after four or five years. By that time the plants will have begun to impoverish the ground. Some, such as delphiniums, may need to be replaced by new plants, while others will be better for dividing and replanting. In the original planting of a border with small plants or divisions purchased from a nursery, it isn't wise to go to the expense of buying enough plants to produce a completely mature effect or solid mass the first year of planting. If, however, you are redesigning and replanting your border and have, for example, large matted clumps of perennial phlox, it is better to divide each clump into three, four, or five good pieces, distributing them evenly through the drift so that in a short time they will grow together and become a single unit. However, it is desirable to do some dividing at the time of replanting so that the shape of the drift is more apparent than the shape of individual clumps.

Plants in Group 3 are so slow-growing that it is difficult to get an immediate effect with them. (See Group 3 drawing.) The only thing you can do is to place them far enough apart so that they will be properly spaced when they reach maturity after eight or ten years of growth. This means that there are bound to be gaps between young plants just bought from a nursery. These should be filled in with annuals or bulbs which can be reduced in number and ultimately eliminated as the peonies grow together. The shape of the drifts the first few years will be indicated more by the filler material than by the permanent planting. Of course, bulbs and annuals may also be used in the border in areas especially allotted to them, and drifts of color may be followed in summer by drifts of annuals. However, that is quite a different thing from using bulbs or annuals as temporary fillers between slow-growing perennials.

Planning your herbaceous border in this way gives you an intelligent approach to the problem of spacing, thus assuring you of a good measure of success.

12

drifts

WHAT ARE drifts?

An anecdote will explain this garden term better than an actual definition. A student and client of mine had tried vainly for some time to explain to her unimaginative gardener that she wanted things planted in drifts. He didn't get even a glimmer of light. Then one day she remembered that he was deeply religious, and so she went to him and said, "Eric, does God ever plant in rows?" He thought hard for a few moments before replying. "Oh, no, God—He plants with the wind —never in rows." "Well," she said, "that's what I want you to do— plant with the wind, not in rows!"

Unfortunately the commonest practice is to group flowers by planting them in rows—usually parallel to the front of the bed. If the bed is straight the lines are often straight, and if the bed is curved the lines are often curved. In the formal garden, which is designed as a geometric pattern, planting in lines is frequently the most satisfactory arrangement. However, in any informal garden where you don't consciously wish to stress a definite and distinct geometric pattern, planting in lines is undesirable. In fact, more often than not it is a confession of failure.

Probably you are asking, "Well, if you don't plant in lines, how do you plant—in squares, blobs, circles, or what?"

The answer is—you plant in drifts.

The method of drift planting seems to be a revolutionary idea to many people. Consequently they are unwilling to abandon their old border plantings. But the theory of drifts is really not revolutionary at all. It is a simple and logical treatment evolved by applying generally accepted principles of good design. It is not *copying* nature; rather it is becoming aware of the meaning of lines of natural force.

Can you draw your own drifts? You can, indeed.

Have you ever studied the way snow drifts up against a fence or other obstacle? If so, you will have noticed that during a heavy fall with little wind the snow forms a bank at an angle, like this:

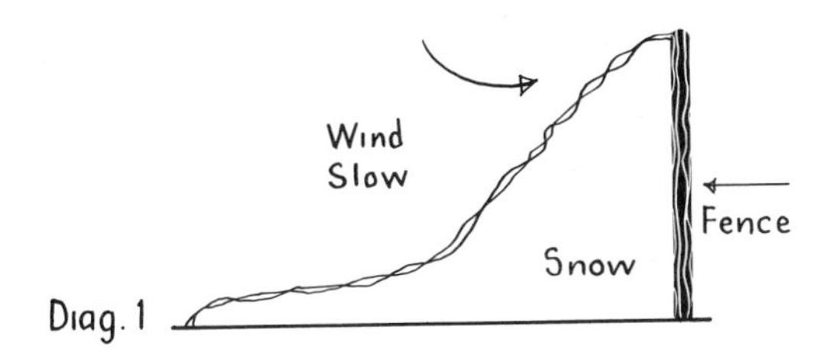

But if there is a fairly strong wind, the snow is driven to form an angle, like this:

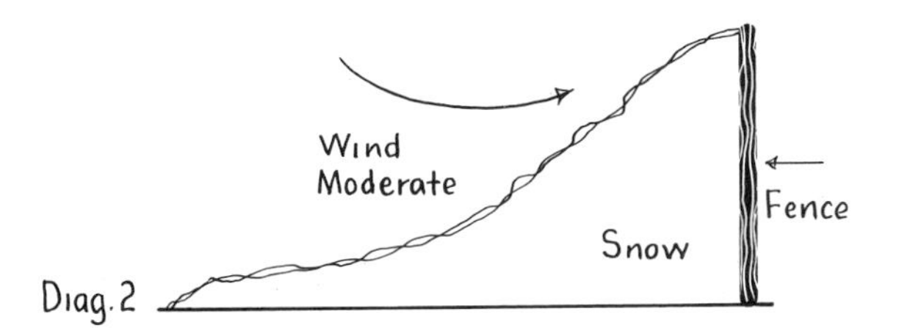

A gale will build the drift back to an even narrower angle, like this:

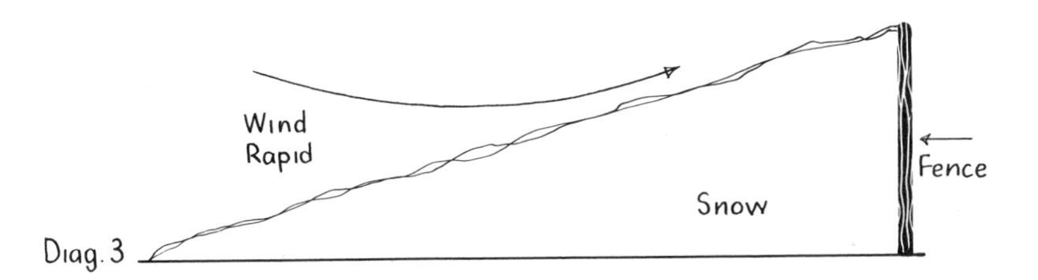

Each of these snow drifts is the product of the forces which created them. We can see that diagram 1 represents slow movement in the direction of the arrow, diagram 2, faster movement, and diagram 3, rapid. Now the snow drift is standing still, but it actually suggests movement. In a certain sense we can say that it has movement. Equilateral triangles, squares, and circles are static figures, not moving in any direction. But if you pull out one corner of a triangle, it begins to have movement and direction, like this:

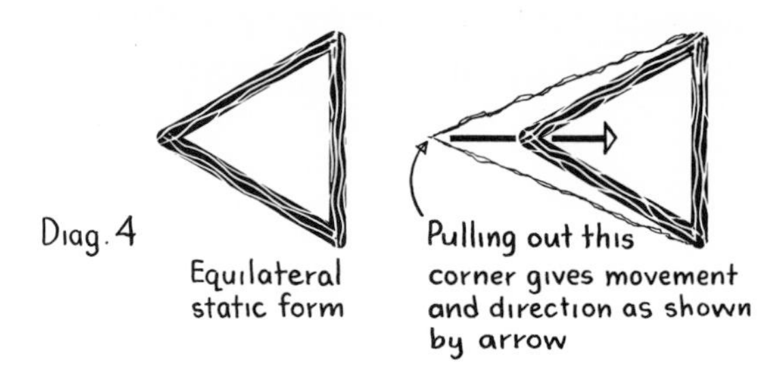

Also a square, if it is changed into a rectangle, has movement and direction, but it does not have as much variety of direction as a triangle. It indicates movement like this:

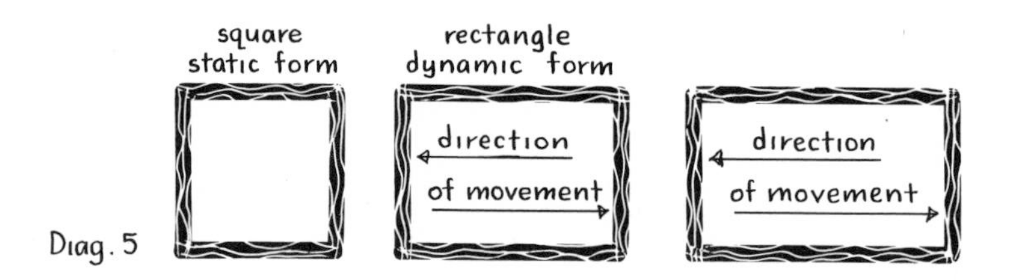

Similarly if a circle is flattened out into a perfect oval, it has a limited sense of movement, but an egg shape indicates definite movement and direction. For example:

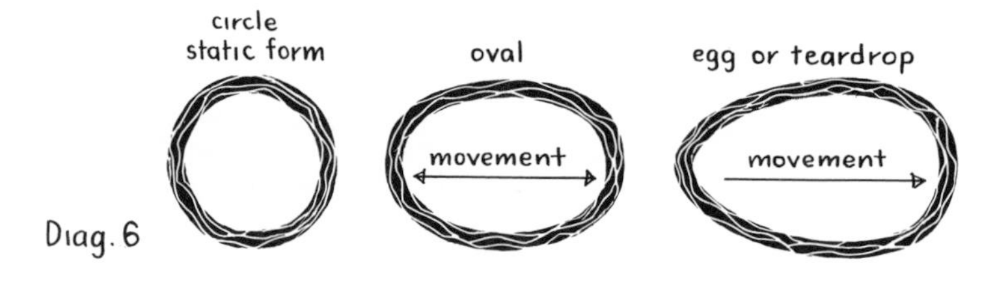

If you notice a drift of fallen leaves in the autumn, you will find that it has interesting curled and swirling outlines and is not usually arranged in as severe a triangle as the snowdrift. So, using the triangle as a basis, we soften its lines by taking a point at the center of the triangle and draw in lines to each of the three points as follows:

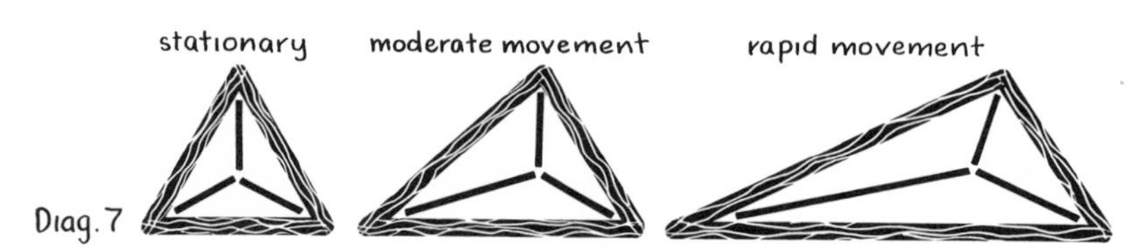

Then change each of these lines to a curve starting from the central point so that each of the curved arms is bent in the same direction. The tip of each curve should be pointed either clockwise or counterclockwise, like this:

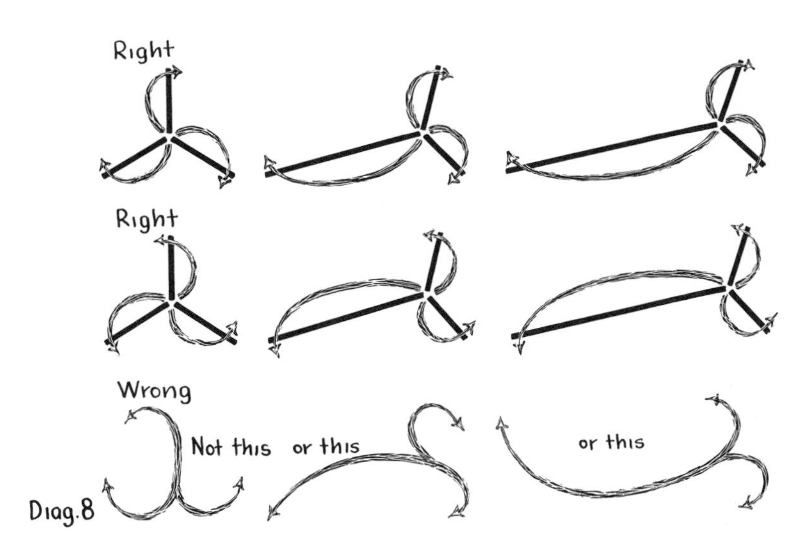

Now build the form of your drift around these three structural lines thus:

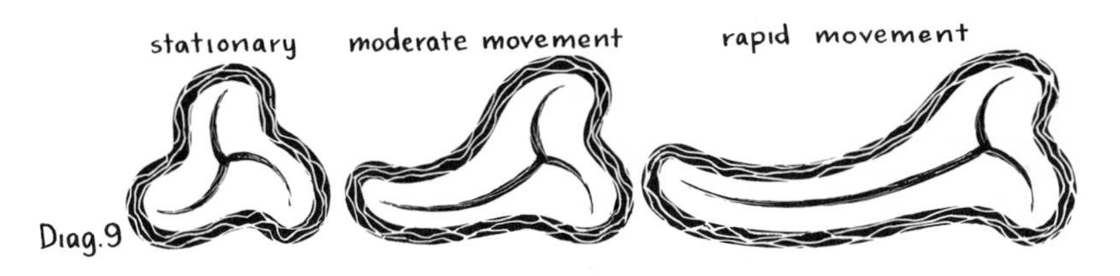

Next, to translate these drift forms into planting, you could place the plants something like this:

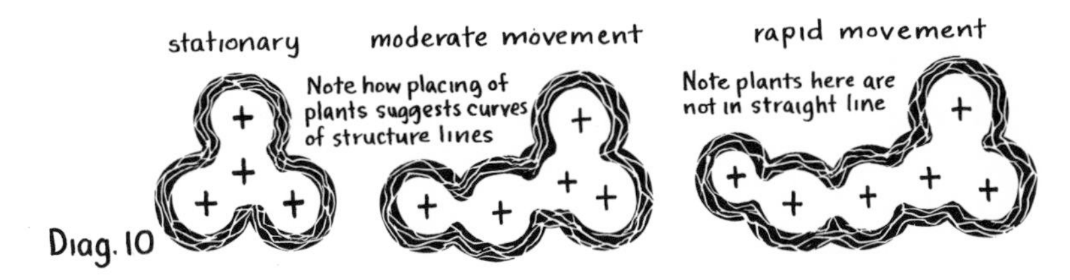

The above series of diagrams gives you an understanding of how these drift forms are evolved. However, this does not mean that you necessarily have to go through this process of working from triangles every time you draw a drift. But unless you understand the steps by which the drift is evolved, you would not be able to draw effective, balanced drifts and place plants in them so that free-flowing movement would be clearly discernible in your planting.

The next thing in applying this to your garden would be the size of the individual drift in relation to the whole area. You need to watch against the tendency to get the drifts too small. It is much better to have a few large, simple ones than to get into a complicated network of very small groupings.

Examine the diagrams in Chapter 13 and you will see how these drift forms have been combined and you will be able to understand now how their arrangement establishes a very definite sense of movement. Notice the absence of any lines of borders or edgings which are so commonly and wrongly used in plantings of this sort. They are not needed to tie the planting together when you use related drift forms like these. Too often a flower bed looks like a loose and bulging bundle awkwardly tied together by a line of edging plants. Once you have learned to draw drifts and combine them, your planting will hold together so well that it will never need a border.

The drawing of drifts is both simple and fascinating if you will take the trouble to study and follow the simple principles outlined here. But remember there is nothing stereotyped about it. As you continue to practice you will find that you can develop a style of drawing drifts that is as individual as your own handwriting.

13 coordinating curves and drifts

THE DISTINGUISHING characteristic of drifts is the sense of blending, flowing movement which they give to the design. Therefore, the next step is to combine them in such a way that they move rhythmically in a given direction. The determining factor in the drifts' direction of movement is the curve of the front of the bed. The first thing to consider is how to make a free-flowing curve and understand its movement.

Everyone is familiar with the shape of a teardrop, which has very evident direction of movement:

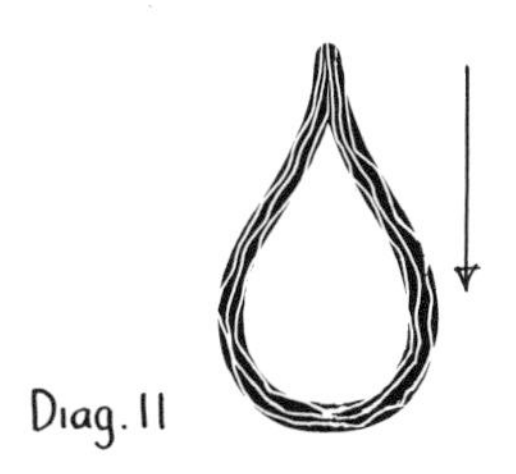

Diag. 11

Now if you cut a teardrop in half lengthwise you will have a curve that suggests movement, as indicated by the arrow:

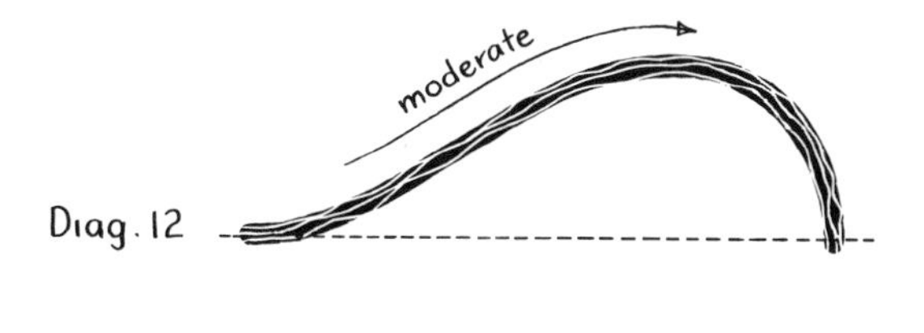

Diag. 12

A short, fat, slow-moving teardrop has a curve like this:

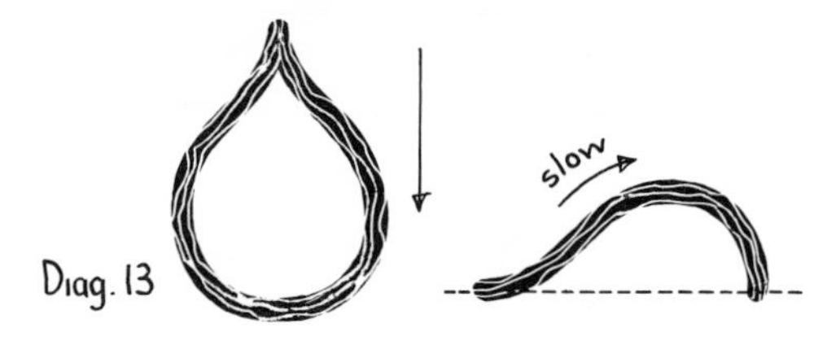

A slender, swift-moving teardrop looks like this:

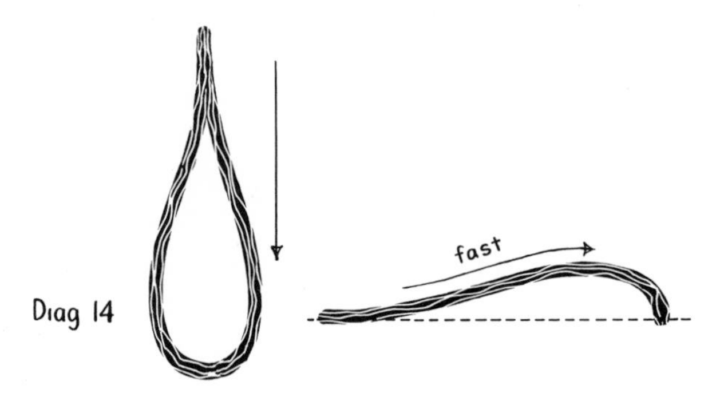

Now let's translate this to curves in your garden. Suppose you're planning a bed with a curved outline and, after careful consideration, you decide on a curve like this:

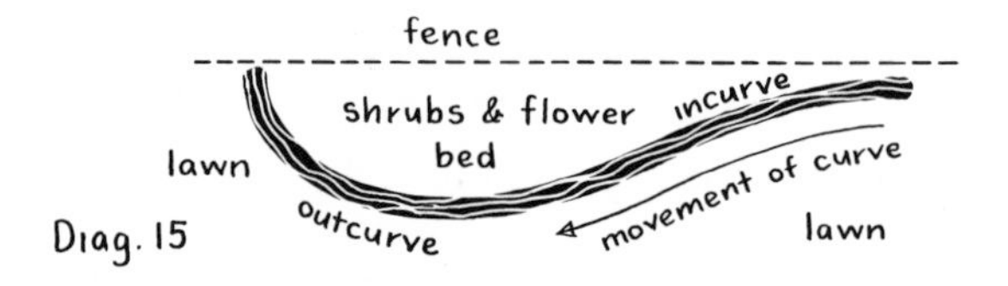

We can say that the curve is moving in the direction indicated, even though it is physically a fixed line on the ground. Thus the simple rule is that drifts should always move from incurve to outcurve. In other words, drifts follow the line of force shown in the curve.

If you are making a curve in the corner of your property, you might evolve a double curve like this:

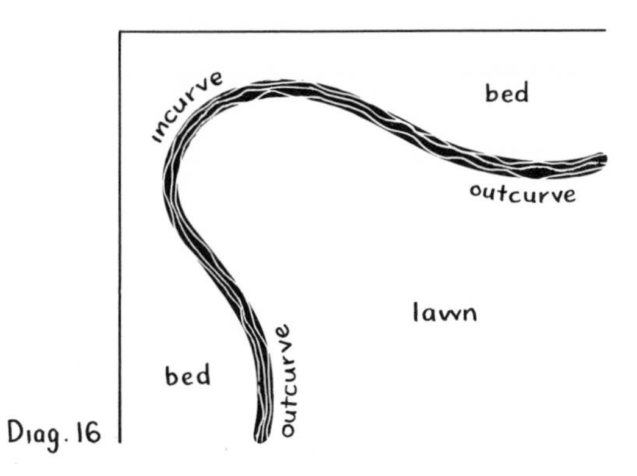

In such a case you could arrange your drifts to show lines of movement as follows:

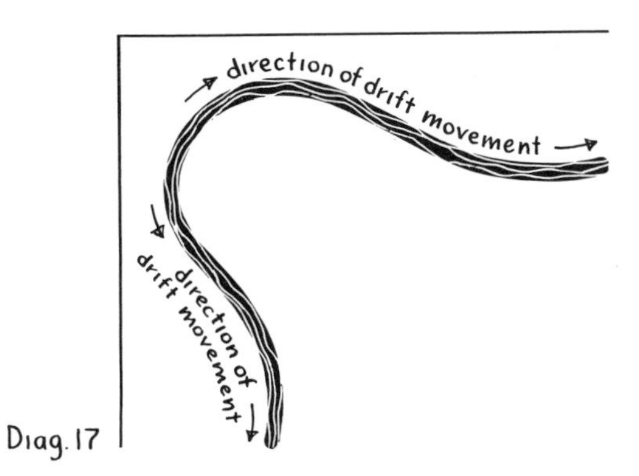

You will find that this works out very well in grouping drifts. Where you have a long, shallow, swift-moving curve you will use swift-moving drifts, which also are long and slender and so fit in perfectly, like this section of border:

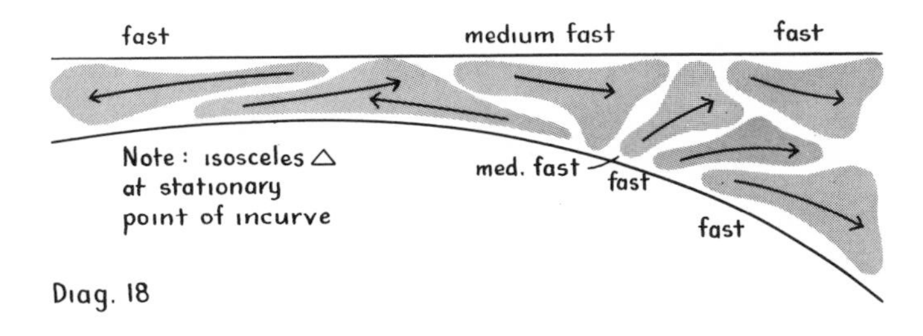

Similarly, when you have a short, deep outcurve with slow movement, your slow-moving or stationary drifts fill in conveniently behind this bold curve:

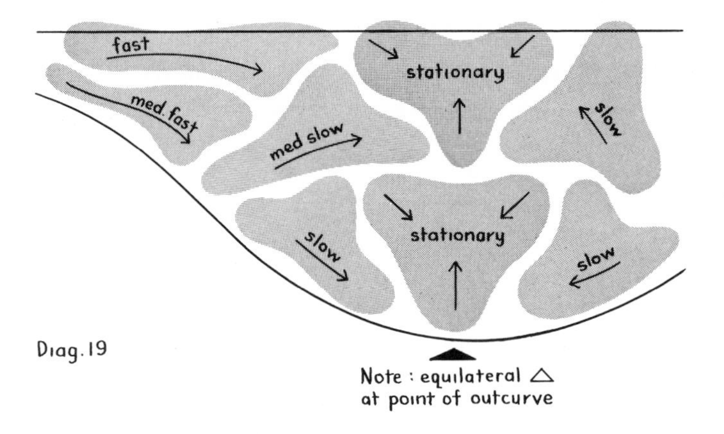

See how well this works out in relating the width of the drifts to the width of the beds. Where you have a long, shallow incurve, the swiftly moving drifts will be long and narrow. Where they move more slowly, they will be shorter and broader. Thus there is a very practical relationship between the widths of beds and drifts.

In an informal garden you will usually end up with a series of incurves and outcurves which could have infinite variation but which, perhaps, might look like this:

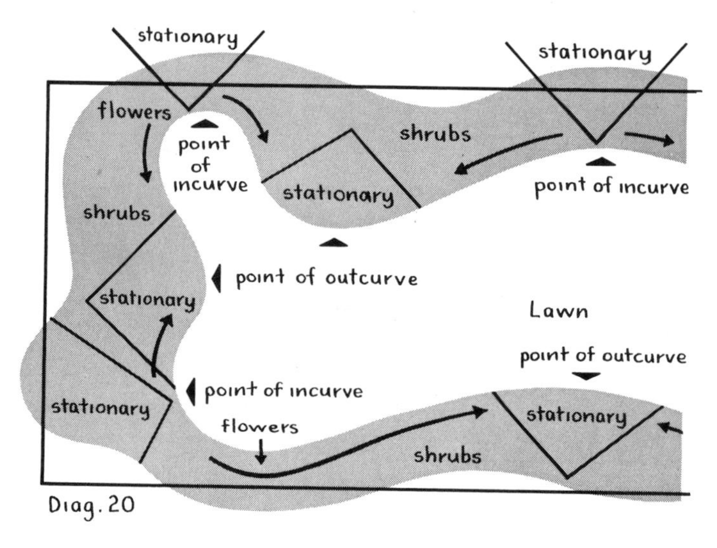

You will see that there is a point at which each outcurve reaches its greatest width and recedes in either direction from that point. Similarly there is a point in each incurve from which it gradually comes forward in either direction. It is at this point that the change in direction of the drift flow occurs. Consider these points as stationary or fixed points and arrange each drift so that it flows from the point of deepest incurve in the general direction of the point of greatest outcurve. In each case you set up the flow of your drift between those points, always moving from incurve to outcurve.

Diagrams 19 and 20 show that at the point of incurve and the point of outcurve there are stationary drifts, that is, drifts which do not move strongly in either direction. Between these points the drifts have definite speed and direction. (Note the drifts marked fast, medium fast, slow, and stationary.)

Often at a point of incurve the shape of the drift is based upon an isosceles triangle which moves sideways in either direction. (See diagram 18.) Because the bed is usually narrow at the incurve you "flatten out" the equilateral triangle to make an isosceles triangle. But when you have an ample width of planting bed provided by a bold outcurve, there is room for either a fully equilateral triangle or else a slight modification of it.

In diagram 20 note how the perennials are set in bays enframed by the shrub groupings and that the shrub groupings come right out to the edge of the beds at the point of outcurve. This also tends to strengthen the same rhythmic movement. Place the heaviest foliage—large-leaved, broad-leaved evergreens such as rhododenrons or laurel—in the stationary area of the outcurve, and place deciduous shrubs at the back of the incurve. This leaves the crescent-shaped areas in the incurves in which to mass the color (flowers). As you look into the garden you see three deeply set bays of flowers framed on each side by a bold outcurve so that each bay becomes an attractive pictorial composition.

Now you can see how every element of the design is coordinated in rhythmic movement. Everything "moves" from the point of incurve to the point of outcurve. The drifts move, and the shrubs move from lightest to heaviest. All of this is related to the movement of the curve at the edge of the bed. The beauty of this type of treatment is that it gives you complete freedom to develop your own taste while still following these simple, basic rules of movement.

Variations of this type of treatment are unlimited, but in working out such a scheme watch the following points:

1. Be sure to use bold curves. One common weakness of this type of planting as it is usually practiced is shown in diagram 21a. The curves are much too flat, presenting feeble variations on the rectangular line of the back yard. It is true that there are

more square feet of lawn and less of shrubs, but actually the area as a whole will look smaller than in the correct solution. The curves are such an ineffective attempt to camouflage the lines of the lot that they make the smallness of the lot more apparent. Note that in the correct solution the curves are so arranged that a bold outcurve corresponds to a receding bay across from it. (See diagram 21c.) This important point has a great bearing upon achieving a sense of spaciousness. Outcurves opposite outcurves would pinch the area into virtually three separate sections. (See diagram 21b.) Corresponding curves, however, give a sense of spaciousness. These bold curves, when supported by banks of trees and shrubs, create the structure of the garden.

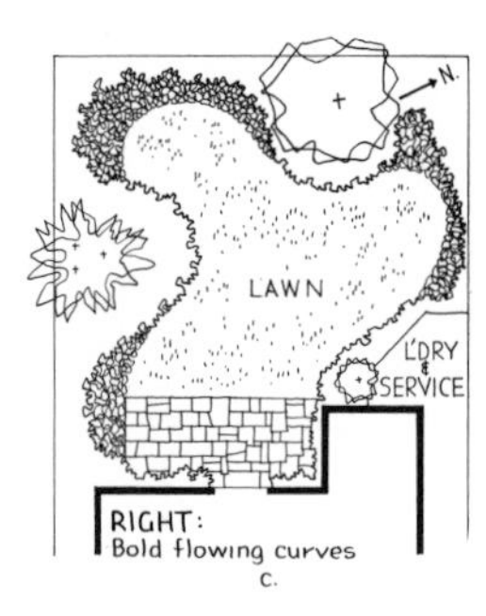

Diag. 21

2. Relate the height of the planting to the width of the bed. As a general rule the height of mature planting should be about one and a half times the width of the bed. For example, when the bed is ten feet wide, the planting should be about fifteen feet high; when the bed is four feet wide, the planting should be about six feet high. This is just to give you some idea of what to plant and should never be slavishly adhered to.
3. Since the bold outcurves automatically become the high points in your planting, place the widest, and consequently the highest, points of planting so that they will occur in just the right position to screen out either undesirable objects or overlooking windows that invade your privacy. When you plant to screen off unsightly objects, try to enframe some lovely distant scene—a tree in the distance, the mountains, your neighbor's garden, or anything that will carry your eye beyond your own small plot

and make it seem more spacious. Remember that the skyline is your horizon and boundary—not the edge of a fifty-foot lot!

4. If it is not possible to screen out everything objectionable from all points in the garden, decide on the most important spots for privacy. This may be the living-room windows or an outdoor terrace.
5. Note that high points or outcurves are not used at the corners of the lot. The piece of lawn cutting in deeply toward the corner greatly increases the illusion of depth and does not diminish the privacy gained next to the house.
6. The bold outcurve by itself won't give depth and spaciousness unless it is strongly supported by high and relatively heavy planting. Always use the heaviest foliage (shrubs with the largest individual leaf) at the center of the boldest outcurve and the weaker and lighter planting in the bays.
7. The shrubs at the outcurve should be well-dressed down to the ground. Don't place a bed of herbaceous planting in front of the outcurve. Let the line of shrubs come right to the front of the bed at the widest point. Either annuals or perennials used at this point, while they may make a pleasing picture in the summer, produce a very undesirable winter effect, leaving a bare, flat space right where the curve of the shrub bank should be the boldest.
8. You will notice that in the plans a tree or group of trees is shown pretty much in the geographic center of each of the outcurves. This should be taken as a basic rule. It gives accent and focal point as well as additional height just where it is needed. For each position plan a tree which, when fully grown, is at least one and one-half times, and preferably not more than three times, the widest portion of the bed.

curves and contours

14

In countries of the Old World—England, Italy, France—small gardens, large estates, or farms give you the feeling that people have worked with close understanding of, and affection for, the land. The houses snuggle into the landscape; the ground lies either in a pleasing, flowing contour or is walled and terraced in such a way as to make the utmost of the land. Is not this one of the signs of a mature indigenous culture? One of the underlying needs of landscape design in America is this sensitive understanding of the ground from which the garden is to spring. That America can superbly meet this challenge is shown by the splendid development of contour plowing to eliminate the threat of erosion in large agricultural areas. Here is an understanding of contours on the grand scale. Farmers who have been educated to contour plowing are now aware of every curve of the land. They have stopped planting in straight lines and rectangles. Although working from an intensely practical viewpoint, they have arrived at a poetic beauty of form that springs from function. (See figure 41.) Here perhaps lies the beginning of America's awakening to the beauty of curve and contour that it is possible to achieve in our gardens.

To many people contour lines are nothing more than pleasant but meaningless curves on a piece of paper. Actually they are the blueprint of the sculptured surface of the ground. A contour line is a line connecteing all points on the same level. The ring around the bathtub is a contour line! The contour plans in the illustrations are simply what you would see if you were looking straight down on rings in your bathtub—or in other words, a plan view. (See contour drawings.)

You may not be aware of good contours in a garden until you learn to observe them. But if you are at all sensitive to beauty you will detect the feeling of unity, spaciousness, and flow which good contouring provides. Utilizing natural contours, modifying them, or creating new ones is an aspect of garden design that corresponds to true, functional design in contemporary architecture. The truly functional design is often the most beautiful, whether it is an airplane or a building, and the flowing curves of lines of natural force (nature's architecture) are often the most effective. This does not mean that you should copy nature—far from it. But the study of nature's contours reveals to us a new design potential, which up to the present has by no means been fully utilized in gardens in this country.

Even that which is commonly considered as "flat" country usually has curving contour lines. That which appears to the untrained eye as a flat piece of ground actually may be a gently rolling contour. A city lot which is considered "flat" can often be developed with pleasantly curving contour lines. It is a popularly accepted notion that a lawn should be flat—or level. This is not necessarily so. The notion that you have to forget about contours if you have a "flat" lot is equally false. Both of these misconceptions need to be explained away. If you need a level space for outdoor living—a space for outdoor furniture, barbecue facilities, and so forth—make a level paved area close to the house. However, a lawn area on which a chair is occasionally placed does not need to be level. It can be enhanced by carefully molded, flowing contours. The spurious idea that a "flat" or nearly level lawn cannot have effective contouring is especially pernicious. A slope of even one to two feet in forty or fifty feet may be so modeled as to make a very noticeable improvement over a completely flat lawn.

Compare a piece of ground with flowing curves of contours to one with broken up, man-made straight lines superimposed without rhyme or reason. The harsh, man-made lines contrast crudely with the beauty of gently curving lines which follow the lay of the land. Sculpture your garden so that it will roll and flow without any sudden perceptible break or change of direction. The small garden, especially, needs flowing contours to give an illusion of spaciousness.

The previous chapter showed the development of the incurve-outcurve theory with trees, shrubs, and herbaceous plants banked in relation to the curves. The next step is the relating of the incurve-outcurve theory to the intelligent sculpturing of contours. One possible solution

Aerial view showing rhythmic grace of lines formed by contour plowing contrasted with the unpleasant straight lines superimposed upon the natural contours at lower left.

Looking up the slope

These two pictures give only a faint indication of the beauty of form achieved by a skillfully sculptured lawn. This is very difficult to convey in a photograph, but examine the pictures closely and you will see how carefully the ground is molded. The contours make it seem broad and flowing and larger than it actually is.

Looking down the slope

44

This island of lawn with a simple rock outcropping and clump of bamboo is very carefully contoured. At first glance it may appear to be completely flat, but actually it is a study in subtle gradations of contours. When the driveway was first put in, the patch of lawn was left completely flat. The addition of considerable soil to create curved contours, accentuated by naturalistic rock outcropping, gave it a charm and character befitting the distinctive lines of the house.

45—

Originally this lawn area was in two levels connected by a flat, straight bank. It was recontoured so that the two levels flowed one into the other, thus creating greater spaciousness with a rhythmic flow. Note the slight valley which runs from the upper to the lower level slightly to the left of the center of the illustration.

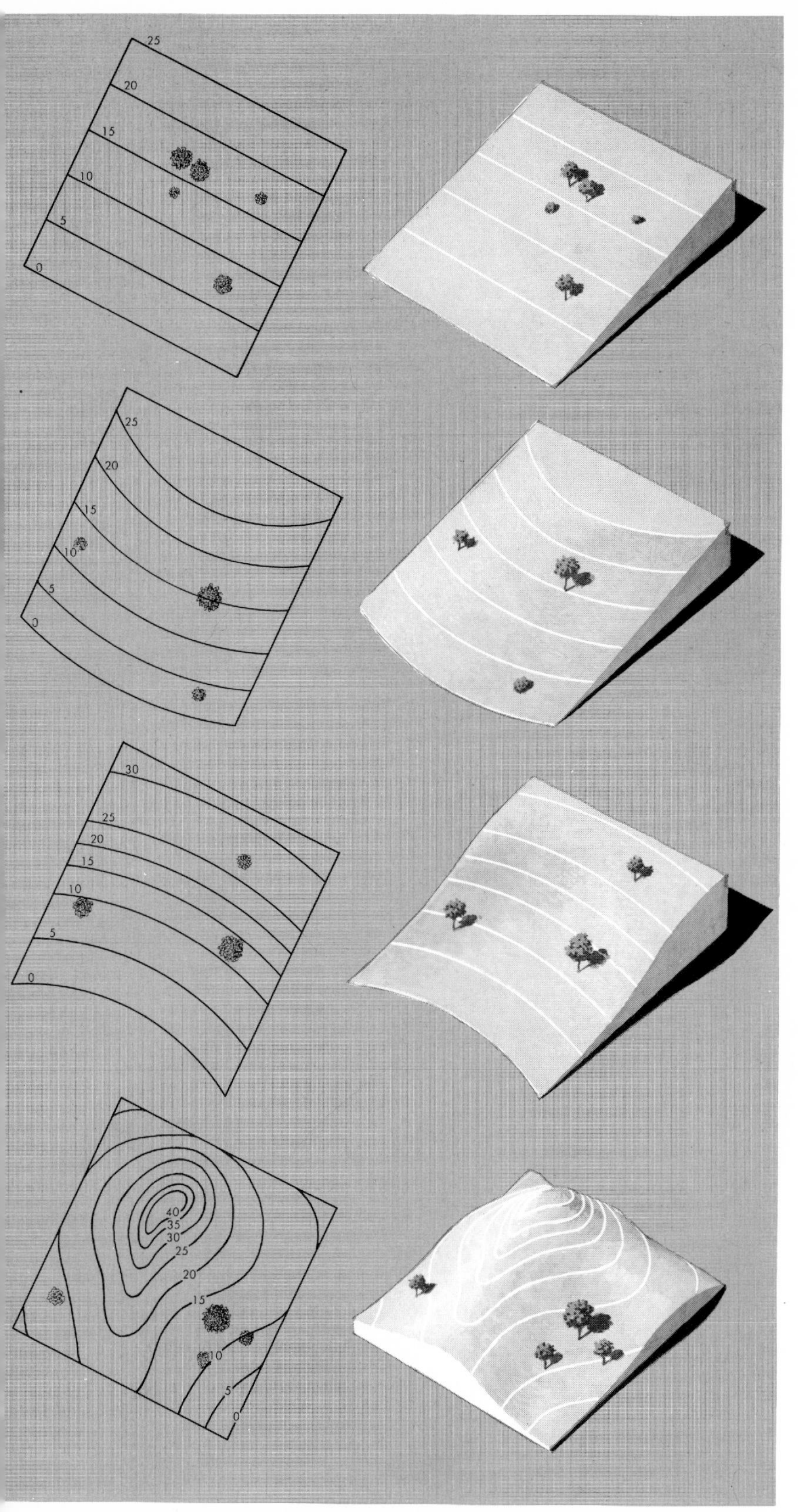

Uniform slope has equally spaced contour lines: Contours from the map (left) have been applied to a third-dimensional model of the ground (right). To use map successfully, you must make a similar transposition in your mind.

Slight ridge is diagrammed this way: When the contour lines curve out toward you, the ground likewise curves toward you. Compare sketch with that of valley shown below.

Valley is diagrammed this way: Where the contour lines curve away from you, the ground curves away from you, forming a valley. Where the contour lines are close together, as with 10 and 25, the slope is steep; where the contour lines are widely spaced, as with 25 and 30, the slope is gradual. You have to watch both the direction of the curve and the spacing between the contour lines to discover the three-dimensional effect which a contour plan conveys.

Diagram of a hilltop: Core of the contour pattern shows highest point. Look for elevation numbers, from 0 to 40, meaning the land rises 40 feet in the particular instance shown. If the numbers were reversed, the diagram would then indicate a hole instead of a hilltop.

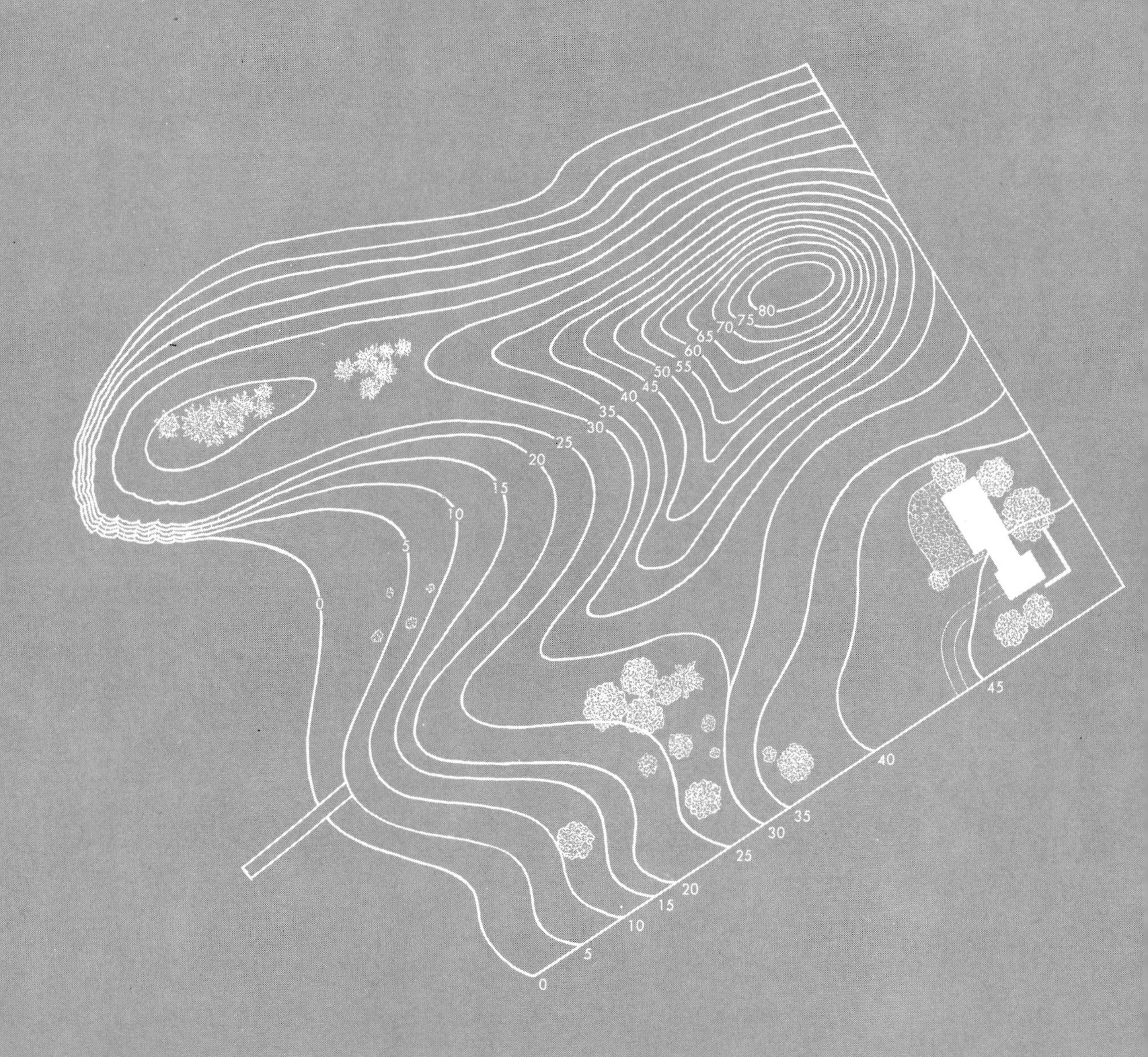

COMPLETE CONTOUR MAP LOOKS LIKE THIS

A contour map of a large area with very pleasing, flowing, natural contours. Examine it carefully and notice the valleys and ridges, the steep and gradual slopes; then try to visualize what it will look like in three dimensions. Now look at the facing page and check up on how accurate your visualization was. Do this several times until you really have the feeling of becoming accustomed to reading a contour map.

THE GROUND AS IT ACTUALLY LOOKS

Examine this illustration carefully and notice how the house and trees show the scale of the area. Compare the height of the house to the difference in elevation between the ground on which it stands and the top of the hill. Look at both sketches and notice that the house is standing on the 45-foot elevation contour line. The house is probably 25 to 30 feet high. There is a slight valley between the house and the highest point of the hilltop. If you were looking across the ridge of the roof of the house on an eye level with it, you would find that the top of the house is almost at the same elevation as the top of the hill. The perspective of the sketch does not fully bring this out, but by comparing the sketch with the contour figures you can get an accurate concept. This exercise in cross reference—referring back and forth to the contour plan and the three-dimensional sketch—shows how much there is to be noticed when you are studying a contour plan.

is to make the curves of the contours and the curves of the bed line parallel. In other words, make the curve of the bed line one of a series of curving contour lines. This would be a good solution for a small "flat" garden that was to be completely enclosed and secluded. This treatment is often used in Japanese gardens noted for achieving a wonderful illusion of space in a very small area. The effect of thus making the line of the edge of the lawn appear to be a contour line gives the suggestion of the grass lying like a body of water surrounded by the shores of your planting. Unless you have seen this done, you can have no idea of what a wonderful depth and spaciousness it gives even a relatively tiny area.

A slightly different contour treatment will have to be used where there is a definite slope. The following treatment is usually best for the average garden. The relationship between the curves and the contours in this case is worked out by having the curves intersect the contour lines at right angles. If you follow this rule, you will find that you will always have the effect of the curves fitting snugly and smoothly to the contours. The rule, then, is that curves and contour lines should be either parallel or at right angles. This is not an irksome rule. If you follow it you will most readily achieve the pleasing rhythmic relationship that you want to get. What you are really doing is coordinating the curves that show in the plan view of your garden to the curves that show in the elevation. It is this third-dimensional effect which is too often ignored in gardens but which makes such a tremendous contribution to the subtle feeling of a perfectly integrated, rhythmic movement of curves and contours.

15 garden color

A GOOD flower color scheme is one of the most sought after and yet one of the most elusive things in the garden design. There could be as many different color schemes as there are people. Many persons jealously guard their prerogative of exercising their own tastes in the choice of color. But there are some basic principles which simplify anyone's approach to one of gardening's most alluring, most exciting, yet most intricate problems—how to use color most effectively.

First of all, the three elements of color are value, hue, and intensity.

Value, sometimes called tone, is the element of color that is too often unnoticed. Failure to consider it frequently spoils an otherwise attractive color scheme. It is the light and dark of a color, that is, the way it might show up in a black-and-white picture. Unless you use a carefully related sequence of color value, your garden will not hold together—instead it will be spotty and patchy.

Hue is the name of the color, such as red, blue, orange, and so forth. It is often thought of as the most important aspect of color, if not the only one, but is definitely second in importance to value. Hues in turn may be classified as cool or warm. The cool hues include the blues, greens, purples, and their derivatives. The warm hues include yellow, orange, scarlet, crimson, and their derivatives. Of course, yellow-green and magenta-purple are really intermediate between warm and cool color. If a little more yellow is added to the yellow-green, it becomes a warm color; if a little more blue is added, it becomes a cool color. Similarly if a little more red is added to the magenta-purple, it becomes a warm color; if a little more blue is added, it becomes a cool color.

Intensity is the relative purity of a color. The pure intense colors of the spectrum band are vivid red, orange, yellow, green, blue-green, blue, blue-purple, purple, red-purple, and magenta. From the standpoint of mixing color pigments you may gray the color or make it less intense in three different ways—by adding black, by adding white, or by adding another color. For example, when you are describing pale pink, you designate its value by stating how light or dark it is. When you speak of its intensity, you refer to how much white and/or other color have been added to pure red to produce the intensity which you call pale pink.

It is an interesting fact that contrasting colors of the *same intensity* do not clash. For example, a pale lavender-magenta will clash horribly with a pure, intense scarlet, but you may be surprised at how well an intense magenta and an intense scarlet will combine. However, intense color is concentrated color and should be used in very small doses in the garden. If you use too large a quantity, it will produce a harsh or jarring effect. The more intense the color, the smaller the quantity you should use. Be aware of the fact that the effect of flower color in the mass is often very much grayed by admixture with its own foliage. The man-made flowers which have been greatly hybridized usually produce a much more intense mass of color than the plants with more naturalistic character. The purpose of hybridization often has been to increase the proportion of bloom and decrease the proportion of foliage.

To apply these three color attributes in a practical way, begin with value. Use dark value at the outcurve and proceed by rhythmic steps or sequence to the light value at the incurve. Decide on whether the light or dark value is to predominate. Then make a rhythmic sequence of value quantity. If you decide to have light values predominate, start with a large quantity of the lightest value, use a smaller amount of medium value (say two-thirds), and an equally diminished amount of dark value. Similarly, to have the dark value predominate, rhythmically decrease the quantity every time you use a lighter value. Either treatment will produce a color scheme with definite character and with great carrying power. The color scheme will not fade out into wishy-washy mediocrity when viewed from a considerable distance. This is illustrated by a comparison of two well-known portraits, one of George Washington and the other of Martha Washington. Analysis reveals that the artist has consciously used a sequence of values. In the portrait of Washington a dark value predominates followed by a smaller amount of medium value and a rhythmically smaller quantity of light value. This produces an effect of great strength and emphasizes the strong, masculine qualities. The portrait of his wife is just the reverse. It uses the largest quantity of light value, a smaller quantity of medium value, and a progressively smaller quantity of dark value. This in turn produces the effect of lightness and softness which stresses the gentle, feminine qualities yet, at the same time, shows strong character. This indicates how value relationships can set a mood. You need to exploit this design principle in planning a garden color scheme. Do you want to bring out a feeling of softness and delicacy, of stimulating and provocative vigor, or of calm, restful strength? Decide just what mood you want to establish. The proper use of value can be the key.

Experience has shown that in making a color scheme with flowers a very satisfactory method is to first establish a sequence of warm flower colors (yellows, oranges, and reds). The full range of warm colors cannot be successfully used in a small area. It would take a distance of 150 to 200 feet of flower border to work in the full range of warm hues. Of course, there is an infinite variety of possible combinations. One scheme that would include most of the warm colors in a space of at least 150 feet is presented here. Commencing with scarlet, work into orange-scarlet and gradually down to orange, rich orange bronze, orange-yellow, yellow, and the pale yellow with just a tinge of green, down through palest primrose to cream and finally white. Then start working up into cream and palest flesh pink, then the pale blue-pink or rose-pink, gradually deepening into a vivid rose-pink and finally rich crimson and magenta.

It is best to use some such gradual sequence of warm flower colors. If you telescope the sequence and try to jump too rapidly—for example, from scarlet to yellow to white within a small space without the intermediate steps—you will lose the effect of a sequence and get a kaleidoscopic jumble of color. This is given not as any hard and fast rule but as the simplest kind of yardstick for estimating the maximum color range you can use within a given space. So, if you have fifty feet at your disposal, you can plan to use not more than one-third of the whole warm color sequence just mentioned.

The cool flower colors—blues, lavenders, and purples—are best used in a series of contrasts to the warm color sequence. These cool colors must be related in both value and intensity to the warm colors

The tulip illustration opposite shows a close sequence of value, hue, and intensity. Tulips do not stand out too sharply nor pull away from their background. The tulips in center foreground are of the variety known as *Blue Parrot,* which has a definite blue-purple tone. The range of the warm hues runs from pale pink to deep pink, with the cool hues from pale lavender to medium purple. There is enough variety to give interest but not enough to produce an erratic or spotty effect. Note how much more interesting it is to use a close sequence of blended colors than just one color.

Note also how effective tulips are when planted directly in front of a vertical background. The exaggerated bloom size and length of stem of the modern hybrid tulips make them dependent upon such a background. Tulips are most effective and practical when used in small segregated areas such as planting boxes near the house, in beds on the edges of paved terraces or patios, or in any level area backed by a fence or wall. Note how several levels of wall and fence have been used here to give height and depth.

Tulip plantings, even though in segregated areas, should be tied into the spring color scheme of the rest of the garden. For example, in this garden there are many trees and shrubs with pink or lavender flowers that are in bloom at the same time as the tulips. This mass of tulips becomes the color keynote, dramatizing the more scattered touches of color throughout the rest of the garden. For summer attractiveness the tulips can be replaced with annuals and bedding plants, such as geraniums, lobelias, petunias, snapdragons, stock, verbenas, and zinnias.

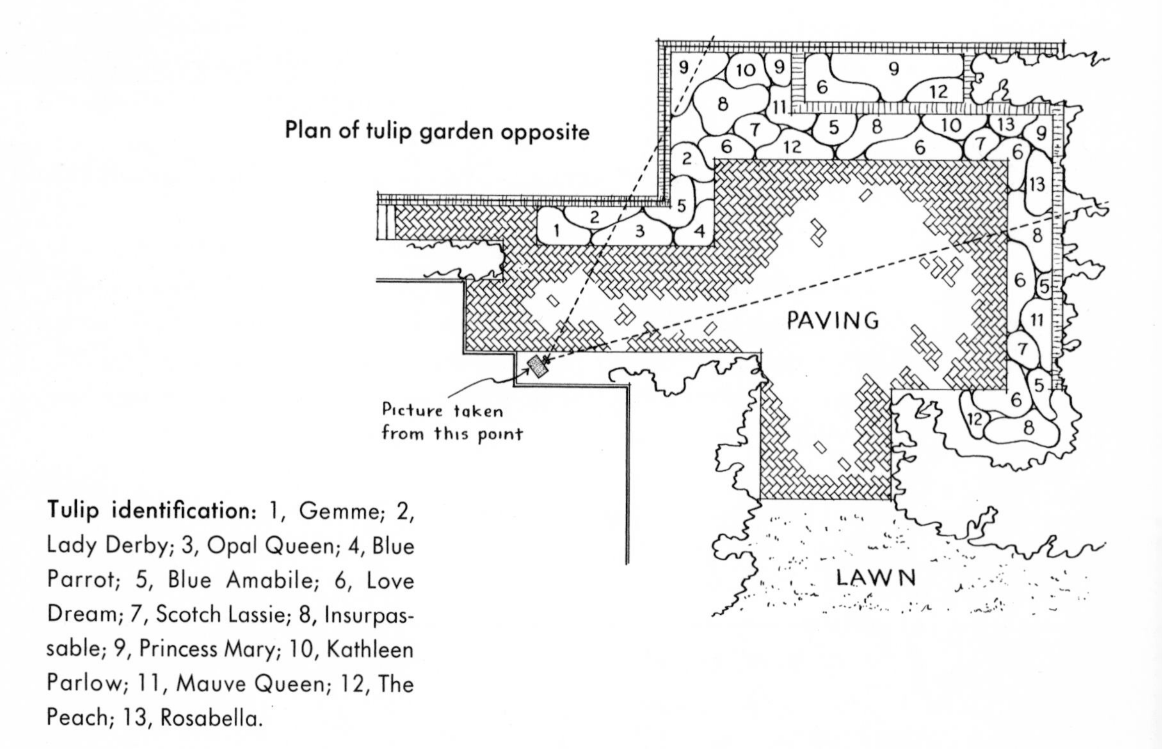

Plan of tulip garden opposite

Tulip identification: 1, Gemme; 2, Lady Derby; 3, Opal Queen; 4, Blue Parrot; 5, Blue Amabile; 6, Love Dream; 7, Scotch Lassie; 8, Insurpassable; 9, Princess Mary; 10, Kathleen Parlow; 11, Mauve Queen; 12, The Peach; 13, Rosabella.

which they accent. For example, you could use a pale blue with a pale yellow, but not a dark blue with a pale yellow, because the difference in value would cause the two to pull apart and break the unity of the scheme. Similarly pale but rather intense yellow would be distinctly off key if you put a soft lavender next to it, which was related in value but entirely different in intensity. The cool colors are like an accompaniment in music that enhances the beauty of a vocal or instrumental solo but is always kept subordinate.

Foliage color also acts as a cool color contrast to the warm flower colors. This predominance of cool color is one of the reasons why an attempted sequence of cool flower colors is usually disappointingly dull. However, you could effectively use a sequence of cool flower colors in the fall if it were placed against a background of the warm color of autumn-tinted foliage.

Give special attention to the relationship which exists between the color of the flowers and the color of the foliage. The soft gray greens of glaucous or woolly leaves are most effective with the pinks, crimsons, and magentas. The vivid yellow greens should accompany the yellows, oranges, and scarlets. Nature usually works it out that way. You need to work out a sequence of foliage color just as conscientiously as you work out a sequence of flower color.

The remainder of the chapter is devoted to examples of the practical application of this color theory to specific garden problems. Plans 4 and 4a (Chapter 11) exemplify the application of this color theory to a spring border set in a deep incurve in partial shade. The colors range from white at the deepest point of the incurve, moving out to pale pink at the closest outcurve (northwest of the incurve), and to deep yellow at the outcurve to the northeast. Note that the range from white to pale pink is a shorter range and occupies a much shorter space than the range from white to deep yellow and orange, and that the spaces which these two ranges occupy is proportionate to the range in color. Also consider the strong naturalistic character that is shown in this color scheme. The flower color is not as solidly massed as it would be in a hot sunny spot. But, as is characteristic of a shady area, it is interspersed with quantities of delicate soft green foliage. The spring color effect is greatly heightened, however, by the interplanting of bulbs, as shown separately in Plan 4a (Chapter 11).

Examine the June border, Plan 6 (Chapter 11). The delphiniums, being the tallest perennials, are placed in drifts at the back of the border against the fence and in the spaces between the lilacs. Each drift is composed of a separate color, beginning with white at the point of deepest incurve of the bed and then going by equal or rhythmic steps into darker tones, from white to pale blue to deep blue to dark blue-purple. In other words, there is as much change in value from the white to the pale blue as from the pale blue to the deep blue, and as much from the deep blue to the dark blue-purple.

Each of the other kinds of perennials is worked out in the same way, starting with the lighter colors at the incurve and building toward the darker colors at the outcurves. There is a series of groupings of peonies, ranging in color from white to pale pink to deep pink to crimson. Lupines and Oriental poppies are each arranged in the same rhythmic color sequence. The iris groupings graduate from white through pale blue to blue and violet-purple. The important thing is that these value sequences all run concurrently from light to dark. A warm flower sequence in an area this size could run either from white through pink to crimson or from white through pale yellow to deep orange or bronze.

Plan 5 (Chapter 11)—the border planting for maximum effect in September—shows a color sequence ranging from light rose pink at the incurve through the deeper pinks to crimson at both outcurves. This pink to crimson range is accentuated and supported by carefully related cool color contrasts of lavender to purple. At one outcurve there is the rich red foliage of the Japanese barberry (*Berberis thunbergi atropurpurea*) and at the other outcurve the dusky purple red of the purple-leaved filbert, making a closely knit color scheme with a carefully graduated sequence of value. While this would make a mass of color sometime in September, this close sequence of definitely graduated color from incurve to outcurve would have strength, movement, and restfulness throughout the whole growing season.

This border presents a solution to the difficult and challenging problem of using flower color to create an illusion of structure without the use of trees and shrubs or architectural background. This problem seldom occurs, but the basic color principles embodied in this example can be used to good advantage in more conventional situations. (For actual plan of this border, see end of book.)

There has been a careful use of the size, shape and direction of the drifts. Individual varieties and colors have been used in separate groups, but note that the groups do not pull apart because they are a closely related sequence of color value. The shapes of the groups suggest movement which coincides with the movement of color. They move toward the outcurves where the dark value culminates (right foreground) and away from the incurves where the lightest value is found. The gradations in height of the drifts at the outcurves is steeper than the gradation in height of the drifts at the incurves, giving the effect of massed weight at the outcurves. Note that there are no ribbon borders of plants lining the edges of the beds. The heights are so arranged that an undulating, contoured effect is produced, which emphasizes the incurves and outcurves of the bed line. The size and shape of the individual flower heads mainly determine the texture and pattern of the drifts. Note the contrast between the spike form of snapdragons and the distinctly round-headed form of zinnias and perennial phlox and the intermediate or semispiked form of stock. Comparatively large individual groups of these different flower forms are used to be in scale with the large area, some of the drifts being ten to fifteen feet long. In a smaller area the individual drifts would be proportionately smaller, but it is always better to work in large, simple sweeps rather than in spotty little patches.

foundation planting

16

THIS CHAPTER coordinates design principles which apply to foundation planting. Some of these principles have been discussed in greater detail in foregoing chapters.

The purpose of foundation planting is:

1. To create a transition between the vertical lines of the house and the horizontal lines of the ground
2. To accentuate
3. To decorate
4. To soften the lines of the house

The first objective cannot always be achieved just by planting. So first consider relating the mass of the house to the ground by architectural construction. A low, rambling house closely snuggled to flat or rolling ground is already well related. It does not have to be tied to the ground. The more strongly vertical a house is, the more "tying down" it will need. Often the extension of the house with a fence or wall of the same material gives the needed effect. The tall house on a steep slope may require a broad terrace held up by a high retaining wall. A completely symmetrical colonial or Georgian structure on level ground may need a generous area of paving or lawn enclosed by a fence, wall, or hedge extending out from the house. If a house has to be related to the ground in any of these architectural ways, don't expect to get the right effect merely with a heavy base planting. The result can never be good.

When you have achieved the best possible solution architecturally, then start thinking about the planting. In foundation planting you are faced with the problem of fusing two design elements—the house and the garden. You must consider carefully which is to predominate. For example, a classical Georgian brick house, with a perfectly symmetrical façade of doors and windows, is a strong design in and of itself, completely dominating the garden scene in which it stands. Therefore, the planting directly next to the house must not compete with it. In such a case of extreme formality the foundation planting might be an unclipped hedge of dwarf boxwood. Similarly a fine old Tudor mansion might look best standing free in a large sweep of lawn with no foundation planting at all. At the other extreme, there is the undeniable charm of a quaint little cottage swathed in vines and half-smothered in soft shrubs. The foundation planting of the average city or suburban garden usually will be somewhere between these extremes. Use the following simple rules as a guide in solving the "usual" foundation planting problems:

1. Bank shrubs at each of the corners of the house to tie its vertical line down to the horizontal line of the ground.
2. The average house does not have a completely symmetrical façade. If it does the central doorway should be flanked with a pair of specimens. When it is not symmetrical, use just one comparatively small tree or large shrub for accentuation beside a doorway—or at any other point in the façade of the house which most needs accentuation. Slender vertical conifers should not be used at the *corners* of the house since this will accentuate the vertical lines at the point where they most need softening.
3. The foundation planting should be one continuous bed, if for no other reason than easy maintenance. Generally speaking, the bed should be wide at the corners and narrow in front of windows.
4. The height of the planting should be from one and one-half to three times the width of the bed. Exceptions to this are the vines and wall shrubs which might be planted in narrow parts of the bed and trained to form a decorative panel of growth. Shrubs which may be trained flat against a wall to very good advantage include *Camellia sasanqua,* many cotoneasters, any of the many pyracanthas, escallonias, and evergreen or semi-evergreen euonymus, and also flowering quince (*Chaenomeles*) and espaliered fruit trees.

Graceful, arching, branching pattern of flowering crabapple (*Malus aldenhamensis*). This small tree makes a pleasing accent at this point in the garden design, and the lines of its branches help to tie the vertical line of the house down to the ground.

Simple planting sufficiently massive to be in scale with house and yet not smothering it. Shrub in front of window to immediate right of entrance is intentionally covering window. Portugal laurel in front of chimney will ultimately reach as high as chimney. Here no accentuating planting was necessary because of definite architectural lines and because house is standing in a grove of fir trees, with dogwoods planted in island in front of house.

An interesting example of asymmetrical balance. Hinoki cypress (*Chamaecyparis obtusa gracilis*) at right of doorway, *Daphne odora* at base of cypress. To the left of door *Camellia amabilis, Daphne odora*, with *Camellia sasanqua* White Doves softly draped against wall at extreme left.

Pleasing effect produced by rhythmic composition, with heaviest mass of broad-leaved evergreen foliage (*Viburnum odoratissimum*) against chimney. Accent of white tulip magnolia (*Magnolia soulangeana alba superba*). Behind it a softening panel of *Clematis montana*. Mountain laurel (*Kalmia latifolia*) at base of magnolia. Left foreground, pink Yeddo hawthorne (*Raphiolepis indica rosea*). Lily-of-the-valley shrub (*Pieris japonica*) extending left from *Viburnum*.

5. The choice of plant material varies with (a) the size of the house, (b) the type of building materials of the house, (c) the range of plant material available in your climatic zone, and (d) the cultural requirements of the plant material itself.

It is important to keep the foundation planting in scale with the house. Too small a planting in proportion to the size of the house will look like an unimportant frill tacked around the edge. Whenever a huge tree stands close to a house and towers over it, thus dominating the entire scene, it, rather than the house, sets the scale and determines the nature of the foundation planting. In such a case you would not use any small trees, either deciduous or coniferous evergreen, since this would be invading the sphere of influence of the one large tree. (See Chapter 5.) Of course, whenever you have an especially large tree to start with, it is essential to use broad-leaved evergreens that are as bold as possible in texture, although the shrubs must not overpower the house in over-all size.

Brick, stone, and concrete houses call for much heavier planting than a frame house. For these, use a bold coniferous evergreen tree, such as pine, for accentuation. Support this strong accent point with a sequence of bold-textured, broad-leaved evergreen foliages. With a light frame house, use a deciduous tree for accentuation, combined with a less heavy sequence of broad-leaved evergreen shrubs. Herbaceous plants are not desirable in a foundation planting because they leave unsightly gaps in the winter time. Similarly deciduous shrubs should not be used except where severe climate does not permit using broad-leaved evergreens.

Cultural requirements are very important. You will need different plant material for each side of the house. This is necessary because one side will be shady and the other sunny.

17 a specific example

THIS CHAPTER presents a specific example embodying the principles which have been outlined in the foregoing chapters. The two plans referred to in this chapter—one the landscape construction plan and the other the planting plan of the whole garden—will be found at the end of the book. The problem calling for a solution was that of a moderately large house on a 60′ × 100′ lot. The front and rear gardens presented two separate and distinct problems. The color illustration on page 21 shows the front garden.

The house was almost completed before the design of the garden was considered. The architect had suggested a low wall across the front of the house, breaking the front slope into two levels. (See dotted lines on plan.) This treatment was abandoned since it would have foreshortened the distance between the front of the house and the street, making the area look smaller. The front of the house had strong asymmetrical balance with a relationship of masses that suggest movement. The ground was sculptured into flowing contours that were synchronized with the curving walk in such a way as to make the most of the pleasing architectural rhythm of the house. The curving outlines of the beds were designed to soften the outline of the house and create as much of an illusion of space as possible. The contours and the curves of the beds were coordinated, a deciduous tree being placed as an accent point in each of the bold outcurves. A pin oak was planted at the back of the house; although it does not show in the color picture it will show above the roof of the house as time goes on, providing an interesting relationship to the other two trees. These three trees, when mature, will set the scale of the area.

Larger-leaved, broad-leaved evergreens were then grouped in three spots, one group at the base of each of these trees and a tall, slender variety of camellia at the left of the front door as the large-leaved nucleus of the third group. A related sequence of foliage size ranging from large to small connects these main points of strength. The planting softens the base of the main window but does not encroach upon it.

Because this front garden is planned to look well the year around, it is composed of broad-leaved evergreen foliages with deciduous trees for accent. However, one deciduous shrub has been added at a point of incurve, *Azalea pontica,* coming up through a bank of evergreen huckleberry foliage. Little scattered drifts of choice daffodils, snowdrops, scillas, and crocuses produce additional color in early spring. The clematis trained across the front of the house flowers in the spring, gives a soft drapery, and at the same time complements the architectural lines of the house. The broad-leaved evergreen foliages massed under the bronze-foliaged plum at the right all have bronze-colored new foliage from spring to midsummer. The other side of the planting, however, is not only in the shade of the flowering cherry but also in the shade of the house. Thus shrubs which thrive in shade and are greener in foliage have been used.

The treatment of the back yard is a solution of a special problem. The area had been excavated to a depth of about seven feet below the original grade. Instead of attempting a pseudonaturalistic rockery to hold up the slope, brick walls were designed to create the maximum amount of space in a limited area. Notice that the walls do not parallel the back line of the lot; rather they were planned to give a feeling of flow by interesting variations in three dimensions. The corners of the walls were so related to the corners of the house as to produce, when planted, a smooth flow of incurve opposite outcurve.

Whether your special problem involves this kind of situation or not, you will want to study the way the planting of this particular garden applies the design principles described in the preceding chapters. The following all-important points were considered in solving this problem:

Privacy. This is the first essential for any area where there is to be any outdoor living, even for a short season of the year. Of course, the longer the season (the year around in some parts of the country) the more important this factor becomes. This privacy may be gained by fences, walls, hedges, trees, shrub groupings, or a combination of several of

51

Japanese flowering cherry *Ukon* at left, *Shirotae* at right. Narcissus and *Helleborus corsica* in bloom in left foreground.

Shrubs from left to right: *Rhododendron Azor*, mountain laurel (*Kalmia latifolia*), *Pyracantha crenulata rogersiana* above wall, and *Camellia sasanqua* trained against wall behind chairs.

52

them. Broad-leaved evergreen shrubs were planted to secure year-around screening and insure privacy. Along the south line there was an existing chamaecyparis hedge belonging to the neighbors which was also used as a background for planting. Had there been no hedge at this point, an attractive wooden fence in some way related to the house would probably have been used.

Illusion of spaciousness. This was achieved in a number of ways. The entire floor of the garden was paved with brick laid on edge in a herringbone pattern, thus producing an all-over, small-scale pattern and texture. It is best not to divide such a small space into part paving and part lawn. Where the climate is relatively damp and cool, choose paving for a usable living area. Where summer heat is intense, a lawn would make for greater coolness. Structural simplicity in the division of space is important, but even more vital and much less understood is the use of plant material to create an illusion of spaciousness. Japanese garden designers, in centuries past, were notably successful in developing this technique, and we can well apply this principle to the design of the small back yard garden today. Basically it is this: the use of rhythmic sequences of foliage texture to suggest much greater depth than actually exists. Notice the illusion of space in figure 51 with the bold texture of the rhododendron foliage jutting out into the paving area. You get the feeling that the garden continues far around the corner beyond the rhododendron. If you examine the plan, you will observe how much smaller the area is than it actually looks in the picture. The picture does not exaggerate the feeling you really get when you are standing in the garden; in fact, it does not do it justice. Broad-leaved evergreen foliage had been used to enframe bays of herbaceous planting, giving the effect of the shrub banks coming toward you and the bays receding. Also at the corners of the house a rhythmic sequence of broad-leaved evergreen foliages has been used with largest leaf and hence the coarsest texture at the corner, the leaf size rapidly diminishing as the planting recedes from the corner. Each of these devices adds its quota to the illusion of greater space.

Using plant material in a structural way. Since there is a very marked architectural structure in this particular garden, the problem was to coordinate the structural use of plant material with it rather than merely to create structure by planting. In every garden there must be points of strength and points of weakness, with a rhythmic relationship and transition between the two. The points of strength feature comparatively large-leaved, broad-leaved evergreen shrubs, and the points of weakness contain herbaceous plants and deciduous vines. Three trees are used in this area as accent points—the key to the planting structure. The largest, a pin oak, free-standing in the paved area, provides shade and sets the scale of the garden. (See figure 56.) Above the wall two different varieties of Japanese flowering cherry have been chosen with as much regard for their branching pattern as for their beauty in bloom. The unusual horizontal branching of the Shirotae cherry helps give depth to the recessed bay over which its branches extend. The fairly heavy broad-leaved evergreen foliage is built up to the base of these deciduous trees to give weight at the base of the accent point. Deciduous vines are used to drape and soften the brick walls. Under other circumstances, where walls were not necessary, a greater number of deciduous shrubs would be needed for background. No coniferous evergreen trees have been used in this area because the space is entirely dominated by the spheres of influence of the three deciduous trees already mentioned.

Year-around interest. This garden features the permanent effect of broad-leaved evergreen foliage. The line pattern of deciduous trees in winter, the blossom of the cherries in spring, and the beauty of their autumn foliage give valuable seasonal interest and color. The broad-leaved evergreen shrubs provide their main display of bloom from early spring to midsummer. This begins with *Pieris japonica* and the sweet vanilla fragrance of *Azara microphylla* (though its flowers are not showy), followed by the fragrance and more conspicuous blooms of *Daphne odora.* Camellias add their quota of gaiety. The one large hybrid rhododendron—*Azor*—was chosen partly for its late blooming. It flowers in this garden at the end of June. As it goes out of bloom the annuals and perennials begin to take up the color theme. Also many of the shrubs featured add even more than bloom in spring with their rich copper, bronze, and red new foliage. This sequence of blooming period has been planned, of course, in this particular garden for its climatic zone. Other materials might be used in other zones to get the same smooth succession of bloom. The effect in spring is enhanced by using bulbs, with a definite segregated area for tulips and with drifts of choice daffodils scattered about the fringes of the shrubs. Tuberous begonias are used with a lavish hand to give an unusual amount of summer color for a shady area.

Temporary and permanent planting. It is necessary to avoid overplanting

53

Broad-leaved evergreen shrubs from left to right: *Myrtus communis, Escallonia rubra, Pittosporum tobira,* and *Magnolia grandiflora.*

54

To left of door, *Camellia Kumasaka,* to the right of door, *Choisya ternata* and *Euonymus japonicus.*

Here the corners of the house are banked with broad-leaved evergreen shrubs—*Daphne odora* and *Camellia Kumasaka,* leaving a small area of flower bed on either side of the French door to be kept filled with color—tulips in the spring and bedding plants in the summer.

A pin oak, free standing in the paved area, sets the scale.

and overcrowding. In general terms the solution is this: space your most important permanent trees and shrubs in the positions they are to occupy in the ultimate scheme. When you first plant them they will probably appear to be widely scattered and the planting will look sparse. You can partly remedy this the first year or two by filling empty spaces with annuals and in some cases perennials. As the shrubs become established and start spreading you can steadily decrease the amount of herbaceous planting. If you know the ultimate sizes of the trees and shrubs you are using and have some idea of the length of time that it will take them to achieve this size, you can plan very intelligently. Another factor to be considered will be that the nature of the herbaceous planting will change as time goes on. When this garden was first planted, it was a hot, sun-drenched pocket. Now in midsummer the bays of herbaceous plantings are almost completely shaded for the greater part of the day.

Cultural requirements for individual plants. These requirements must be considered especially carefully in a very small area like this one. Note, for example, that in every case sun-loving plants are placed in the sun and shade-loving plants in the shade. *Magnolia grandiflora* is planted in the warmest and most sheltered corner and *Pieris japonica* where it gets partial shade. The shrubs along the back line of the property on top of the wall, which is naturally dry and well drained, are ones which usually receive too much moisture in watered gardens in the Pacific Northwest. They are perfectly suited culturally in this plan. Similarly, under the balcony where no rain falls is a warm, dry spot planted with *Choisya ternata* (Mexican orange), which also usually receives too much moisture. (See figure 54.)

Size, shape, and habit of growth of individual plants. Another necessity in achieving a happy restful garden picture is to choose a plant of just the right habit of growth, as well as ultimate size and shape, to fill any given space gracefully. This garden illustrates how readily a planting can be fitted into a narrow space if the right selections are made. Many shrubs used here have draped themselves becomingly against a wall. They have needed a little correct pruning and an occasional support, but nothing more. Among these are *Escallonia rubra,* splayed against the wall immediately to the right of the French door in figure 53 and the *Euonymus japonicus* in figure 54, which is shown spreading out against the upper right of the brick wall at the right side of the picture. In figure 56, photographed in the early spring, you can just barely see the outline of *Clematis jackmanni* trained against this wall, making in midsummer a great splash of rich soft purple which harmonizes perfectly with the pinkish cast of the brick. Cascading down the wall at the right side of the picture is the yellow winter-flowering jasmine (*Jasminum nudiflorum*). The clematis is trained up the wall and the jasmine draped down over it, again indicating an understanding of the way in which these two vines prefer to grow.

In other words, it is absolutely vital in a small area to use just the right plant in the right place, and this requires a thorough knowledge of plant material. For this there is no substitute.

The design value of each type of plant, its naturalistic character, the relationship of plant materials in rhythmic movement of line, pattern, texture, color, and mass—all these contribute to producing a beautiful garden.

No two design problems are exactly alike. Almost every garden presents a special set of conditions, circumstances, and requirements. But the informed designer can solve these problems with sound, logical analysis and thus avoid the pitfalls of stereotyped thinking. The understanding of design principles and their application, as illustrated here, curbs the erratic personal elements and produces a more consistently satisfying design. The more you utilize these principles, the more practical and beautiful the result.

supplementary examples

Figures 57 to 61 show a house and garden that present a very unusual solution to a specific problem. Situated on a windy bluff that all too often makes the view side of the house too cold for enjoyment as an outdoor living area, the house is planned around an open court with glass walls that make indoor-outdoor living both pleasant and practical.

57

The rear of the house gives little hint of the exciting inner court and dramatic front view, but its good simple lines quietly reflect the elegance that is characteristic of the house.

Entrance on opposite side of house is through a little open court filled with shade-loving plants—salal, Oregon grape, sword fern, *Sarcococca hookeriana,* and *Funkia lancifolia.*

Interior court showing carefully restrained planting. On far wall from left to right: *Pieris japonica, Sarcococca hookeriana* immediately below it, *Lonicera pileata* at corner of pool, sword fern, *Camellia sasanqua, Mahonia aquifolium,* and Hall's honeysuckle trailing over window. *Saggitaria* (arrowhead) and *Iris pseudacorus* in pool.

60

Another view of court. Shrub in foreground against window is *Magnolia stellata*. Other plants identified in figures 59 and 61.

The handsome madrona (*Arbutus menziesi*) dominates the scene. At its base salal, evergreen huckleberry, sword fern, and *Sarcococca hookeriana*. Against the far wall salal at base with tracery of climbing hydrangea (*Hydrangea petiolaris*). Note flower bed in foreground which provides for bedding out plants to give spring and summer color.

Figures 62 to 65 present a garden on a comparatively level, triangular corner lot. Again it is an individual solution, but the problem occurs in varying forms in most gardens on level lots.

62

Looking toward house from corner: pin oak at left will gradually become very large and set the scale of the area. Note how the planting ties the house down to the ground and carefully relates the rolling contours of the lawn and sweeping curves of the shrub banks to the asymmetrically balanced mass of the house.

Detail of patio showing pattern of vines and foundation planting. *Wisteria floribunda* trained in long, horizontal lines carefully spaced. Summer flowering jasmine (*Jasminum officinale*) on wire frame at right. Soft foliage at base of chimney is a drift of Chinese sacred bamboo (*Nandina domestica*). On wall to the left of swing, *Azara microphylla*.

64

Looking out from walled patio to point of triangular lot, showing rolling contours of the lawn related to the vigorous flowing curves of the bed lines. Note the boldest mass of the broad-leaved evergreen foliage at the outcurves, the flowers set in the receding bays or incurves. The walls of the patio shown in the foreground and the banks of shrubs are so placed as to give privacy from the street while still retaining an open feeling in the whole design.

65

Detail of foundation planting. Left to right: Japanese privet (*Ligustrum japonicum*), evergreen huckleberry (*Vaccinium ovatum*), *Azalea altaclarensis*, Oregon grape (*Mahonia aquifolium*), and *Photinia serrulata*.

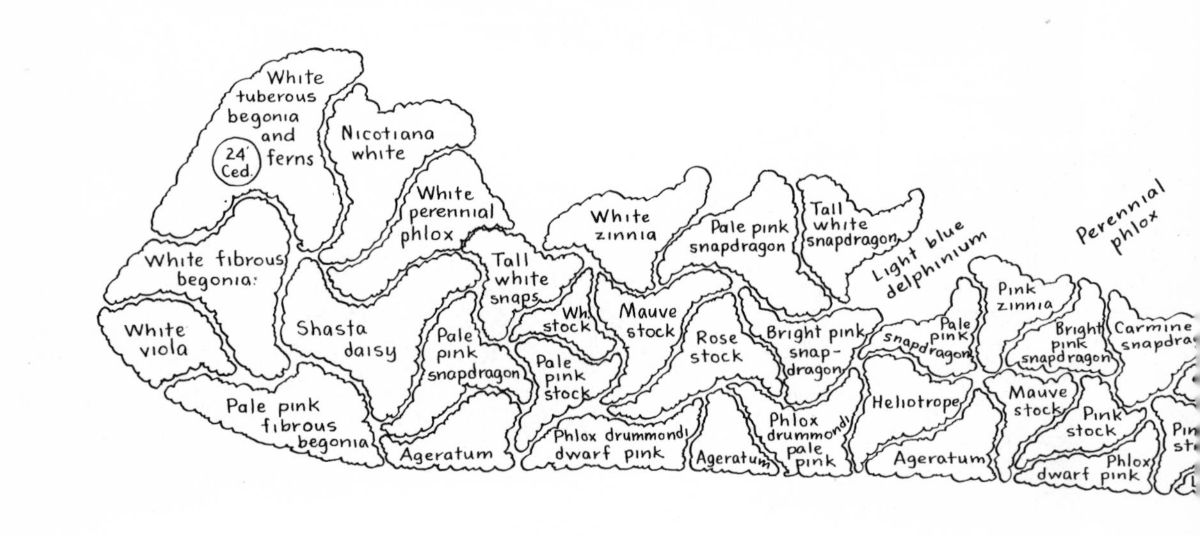

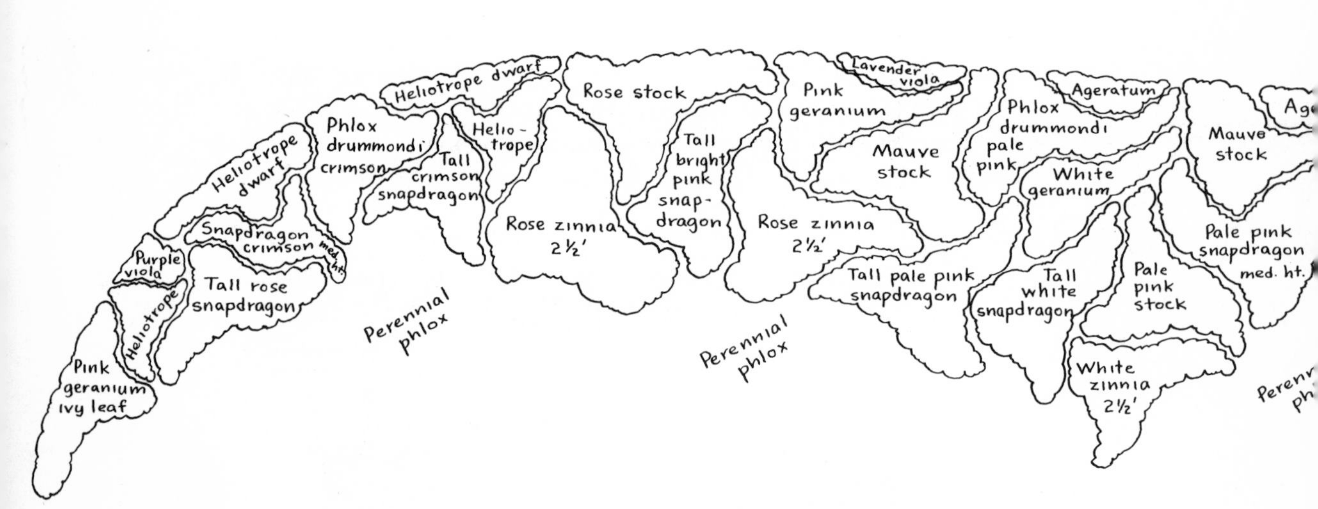

PLANTING PLAN FOR ANNUALS AND PERENNIALS (Chapter 15)

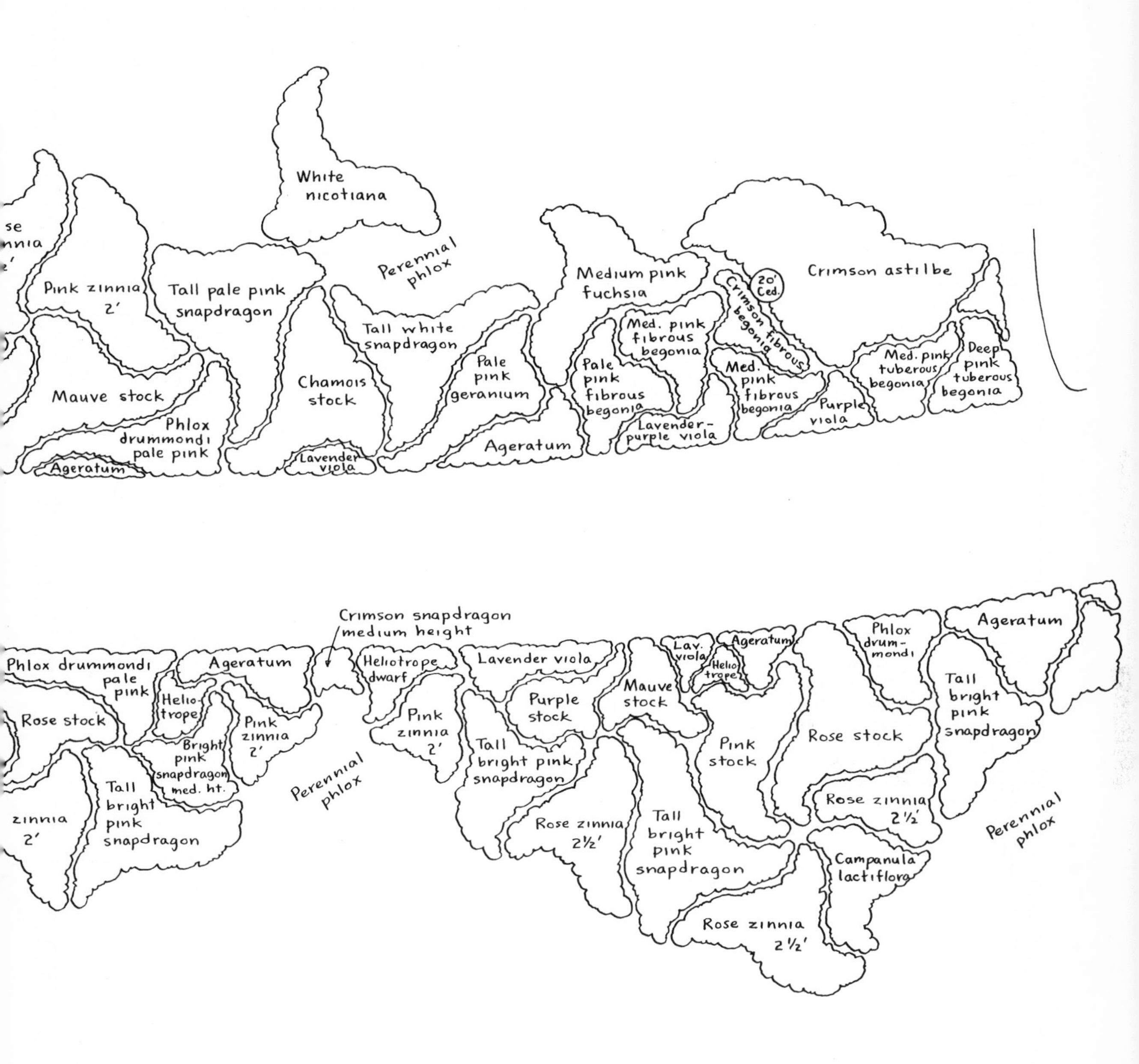
White nicotiana
Perennial phlox
Pink zinnia 2'
Tall pale pink snapdragon
Medium pink fuchsia
Crimson astilbe
20' Ced.
Crimson fibrous begonia
Tall white snapdragon
Med. pink fibrous begonia
Mauve stock
Chamois stock
Pale pink geranium
Pale pink fibrous begonia
Med. pink fibrous begonia
Med. pink tuberous begonia
Deep pink tuberous begonia
Phlox drummondi pale pink
Purple viola
Lavender-purple viola
Ageratum
Lavender viola
Ageratum
Crimson snapdragon medium height
Phlox drummondi pale pink
Ageratum
Heliotrope dwarf
Lavender viola
Lav. viola
Ageratum
Phlox drummondi
Ageratum
Helio-trope
Mauve stock
Helio-trope
Rose stock
Purple stock
Pink zinnia 2'
Pink zinnia 2'
Tall bright pink snapdragon
Bright pink snapdragon med. ht.
Tall bright pink snapdragon
Pink stock
Rose stock
Perennial phlox
zinnia 2'
Tall bright pink snapdragon
Rose zinnia 2½'
Rose zinnia 2½'
Perennial phlox
Tall bright pink snapdragon
Campanula lactiflora
Rose zinnia 2½'

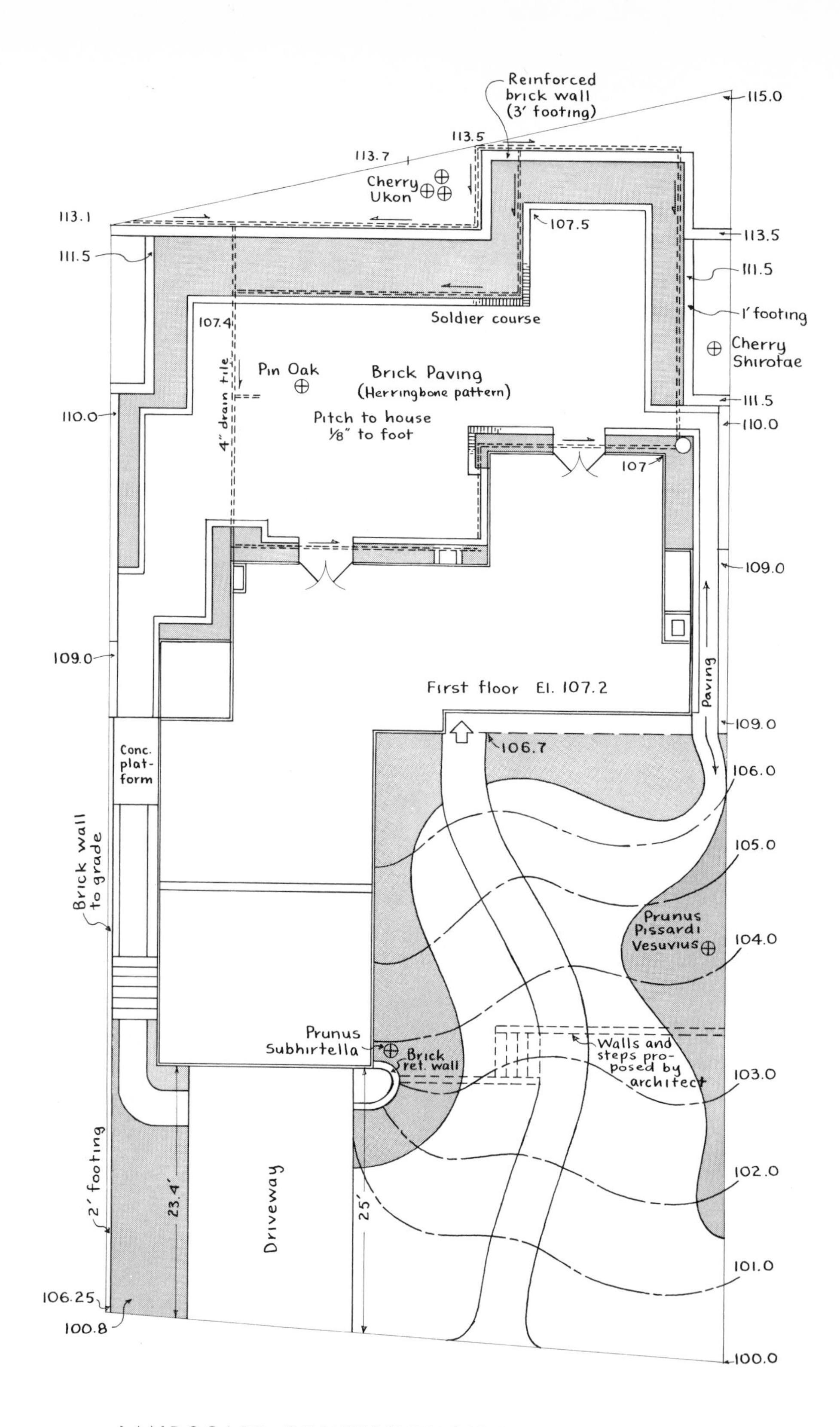

LANDSCAPE CONSTRUCTION PLAN (Chapter 17)

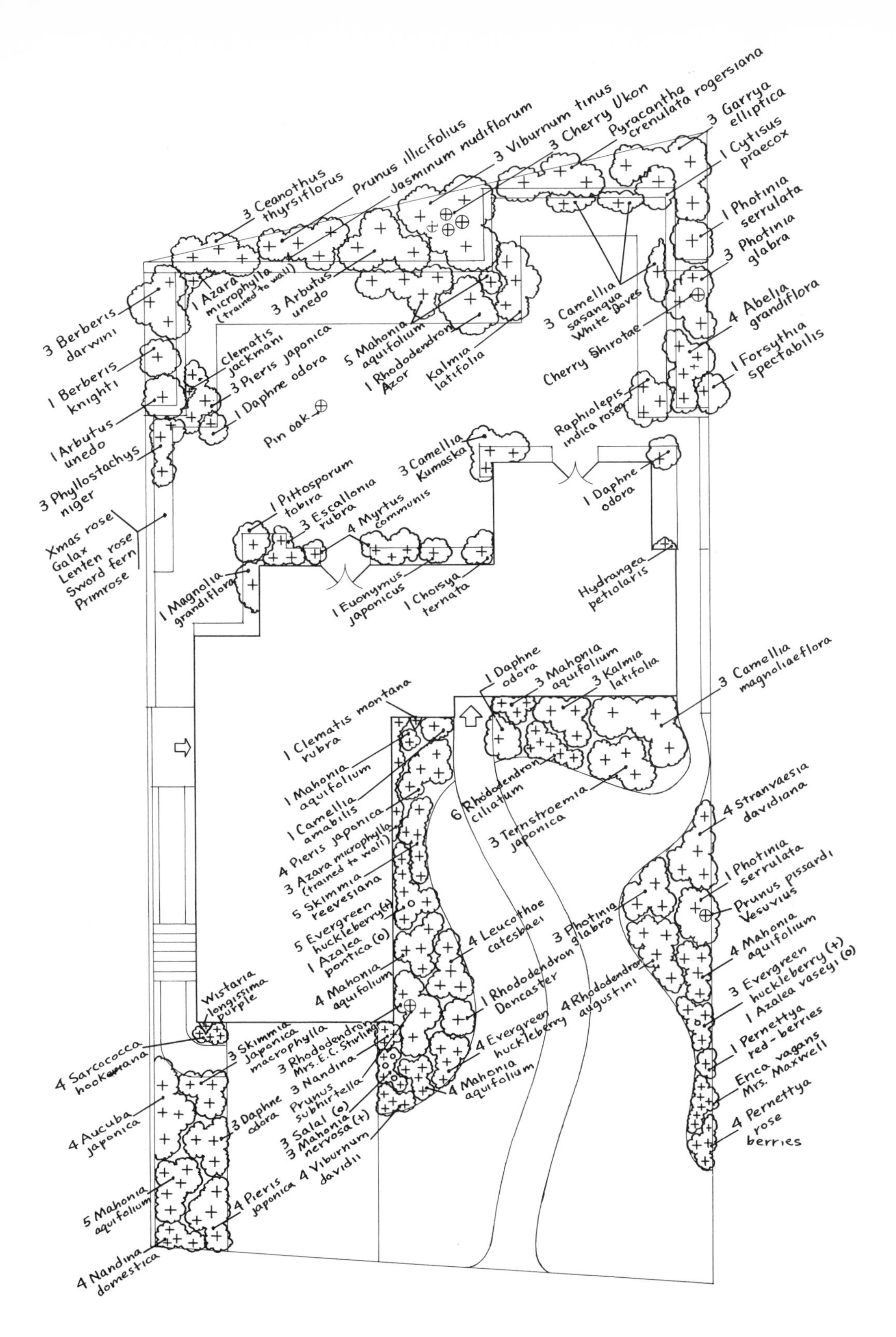

LANDSCAPE PLANTING PLAN (Chapter 17)

credits

photographers· All photographs used in this book are the work of Maynard L. Parker except as noted below:

Dearborn-Massar—flower border (color); O. V. Gordon—fig. 41; Gottscho-Schleisner—title page and figs. 6, 17; John A. Grant—figs. 14, 21, 25, 34, 35, 36, 39, 40; Nyholm & Lincoln—fig. 5.

landscape architects· The landscape architecture illustrated in this book is the work of John A. Grant except as noted below:

Innocenti and Webel—fig. 6; Dorothy Nicholas—title page; designers unknown—figs. 13, 18.

architects· The following architects are represented in this book:

Van Evera Bailey—figs. 7, 8, 23, 28; Pietro Belluschi—figs. 3, 4, 44, 45; J. Lister Holmes—residence (color) and figs. 53, 54, 55.